Yesterday's
Warriors

Books by Mel Marks
Yesterday's Warriors
Jews Among The Indians

Yesterday's Warriors

Mel Marks

Benison Books
Chicago

Published by
Benison Books
333 North Michigan Avenue
Chicago, Illinois 60601
312 750-1450

Library of Congress Catalog Card Number: 98-74416

ISBN 0-9632965-2-3

Printed in the United States of America 6 5 4 3 2 1

Book and jacket design by David Doty

ACKNOWLEDGMENTS

I wish to express my debt to all the officers and men of the 124th AAA Gun Battalion, those living and dead, with whom I served during the Second World War. They taught me, in so many different ways, what true friendship is all about. I feel the need to single out Ed Soares, Bowen N. Smith, the late Ed Harris, and Tony Rodrigues and his wife, Kathy, for having done so much to keep "The On-Target Gang" on target for all these years. I also want to thank Frank Korn for his painstaking editing; David Doty for his first-rate book design; Joe Esselin for his innumerable suggestions on the writing of this book; and Gordon Winkler who, with his bombardier's eye, lined up the cross-hairs on an early draft. And these others: my wife, Mary, my children, Bill, Tom and Patricia, and my five grandchildren. Just having them around was an inspiration.

CONTENTS

Prologue   1

1. Our 54th Reunion in Scottsdale: 5
    Here we are again, still hanging in, Ed Soares still
    leading the charge.

2. Sergeant Joe Snopek: 13
    My favorite tyrant who almost made a
    soldier out of me.

3. Bruce Brodie: 31
    Friends you make on a troop train are friends to
    the end.

4. Bowen N. Smith: 49
    The bird colonel who never stopped marching

5. The Battle of the Bulge: 63
    Even hell has a moment of respite

6. Phil Rodriguez: 79
    We had been friends for 53 years, each of us from
    a different ghetto

7. Jim Oxford: 95
    Our own "Seldom Seen Slim," the Oxnard loner

8. Ed Harris: 103
    Tracer of lost buddies.

9. A Death in the Battalion   111
    Our best kept secret

10. Cortez Hunter: 115
    He fished in Lake Isabella, drank at
    El Rancho No-Got

11. Alvin Huey Long   125
    The unceasingly jovial Oklahoman from Arizona

12. Lost Everywhere in Europe   131
    They didn't give us road maps

13. Our Post-War Variety Show   135
    Shuttered after two performances

14. Captain John Behl   145
    The man who loved liver

15. Earl White   153
    Our last visit together before he died

16. Pancho Contreras   163
    The quiet man who fought in two wars

17. The Bittersweet End of our 54th Reunion: 171
    We never say goodbye

    Appendix   177

PROLOGUE

Early in the Second World War, 750 young men were inducted into an artillery battalion, and I was one of them. We went through training together, were sent to England to participate in the second Battle of Britain, then saw combat in four campaigns on the continent and in due course were sent back into civilian life.

The battalion was disbanded late in 1945, but by an alchemy that has mystified me during more than five decades, our lives were forever joined together, and this book is impelled by my wish to explain what this phenomenon is all about.

If it is strict military history you're looking for, be forewarned that this is not a book about the war. My memory of what happened during combat is much too vague for that. And besides, if you like to rejoice in your memories, as I do, there is nothing celebratory about remembering the havoc of war and its terrible aftermath. Rather, this non-war, war book deals with friendships, the bonding, if you please, that developed over the last half century with my brothers-in-arms and me. These are the kinds of memories that you never want to lose.

Furthermore, this book, I confess, is sentimental, perhaps overly so. How can it be otherwise when you're writing about the men you've gone through combat with and have remained close to for over half a century? How can you avoid sentiment when you regard these men as your brothers, as family, when so very many of them have passed away?

I have attended 50th wedding anniversaries when someone will ask the aging couple to recall their first meeting. So isn't what's fair for them to explain, also fair for me? After all, my comrades and I have been wedded to one another for well over 55 years. Is it any wonder that I can remember when and where most of us first met? The place was Camp Callan, California, where we arrived for our basic training in early March, 1943. From there, we were shipped as a unit to Camp Haan, California, where on May 16, we were formed as the 124th AAA Gun Battalion (Mbl.), an anti-aircraft, anti-tank artillery outfit. Another 116 men, who had just completed basic training at Camp Wallace, Texas, were subsequently to join the battalion.

We were all strangers. With a few exceptions, we were the same age, either 18 or 19. Many of us had not finished high school. Some never would. Most came from Texas, California and Oklahoma, and to the best of my knowledge they did not come from families of means, nor had any of them gone on to acquire great wealth. I can say this about them, however. They were real people then, and they're still real people. They had no free rides in life. And having been brought up during the Depression, they learned to keep a tight grip on their money, except for an occasional fling on the slots in Reno or Las Vegas during reunions.

We remained together for three years, from 1943 until December 1945, fighting our way through France, Holland and Germany as part of the Ninth U.S. Army. We suffered some casualties along the way and a few men for various reasons were either discharged or transferred. Still, for the most part we are the very same group of men who first came together at Camp Callan or Camp Haan. I often wonder what my life would have been like if I hadn't had the privilege of knowing these men.

What's remarkable is that we continue to see one another every year during annual reunions, and sometimes more frequently than that. These gatherings began shortly after our discharges. We don't miss a year. It seems that we just can't stay away from one another. I've asked some of the men what the attraction is but the only answer they can come up with is that they'd attend a reunion even if it meant having to crawl to get there. And some of them have had to do just that.

Between 1968 and 1988, the reunions were in full swing. Nearly a third of the men showed up, their wives in tow. Most had not yet retired. We were in good health. We had some dough. We would drink and play cards and play golf and poke fun at one another. Memories of the war had dimmed, and there was no longer talk about Nazis or Krauts or wartime sexual exploits, but what we heard instead was talk about future retirements and

grandchildren. Ours had been a momentou
had come to the reunions to embrace one
ourselves that we were still connected to the

But by the end of the 1980's, attend
began to drop. Having retired at about tha
living on pensions. The old vitality was g
Relatives began to take the places of the dec
years, attendance has shrunk to around thirty men.

I'm not sure how many more reunions there will be. My
brothers-in-arms say they'll go on for as long as there's at least two
survivors left. But even if our get-togethers don't continue, at least
I'll have my memories.

About five years ago, I decided to pay a visit to some of the
men. I found myself thinking more and more about them. And I
wanted to write a book that would tell the story of our battalion,
the battalion that the men refused to let die. I wanted to find out
what was going on in their lives. How were they coping with
advancing years? And most important of all, what was driving them
year after year to our annual gatherings? Finally, my curiosity
became too overpowering to dismiss. I packed a suitcase and flew
off to California, where so many of the men resided. I then went
on to Arizona and Oklahoma, having talked, all told, with a dozen
or more men along the way — in their living rooms, at their
kitchen tables and in restaurants and bars. I talked with still others
at subsequent reunions. And I continued talking and listening
until I realized that there were other matters implicit in the project. Not only was I trying to get a better understanding of the
men with whom I served but I was also trying to gain insights into
my own behavior during that crucial "growing-up" time. Neither
do I discount the notion that I was also trying to re-create a time
and place that for so long has held such an important spot in my
memory.

The book that follows delineates what I found along the way.

Mel Marks
Chicago, 1998

ONE

Before I showed up in Scottsdale for our 54th army reunion, I had a lot of misgivings. When you get together every year, as we do, you approach these events with foreboding. You wonder if some of the old regulars will make it; and then if they do make it, you begin to worry, just from the look of them, if this will be their last reveille? What's more, you wonder if some of the glory has dissipated, and whether our tattered guidon still hangs together in one piece, and if the pride of victory is still important after nearly a lifetime of celebration. I wasn't sure what to expect when I walked into the lobby of the sprawling resort motel on that hot October afternoon. As you grow old, a lot can happen in a year's time.

The gathering was held in a decaying area of downtown Scottsdale. Some of the exclusive shops and galleries still lined Fifth street and Main street but junk establishments were beginning to creep in from Scottsdale Road. When I walked into the motel lobby, I looked for an announcement of the reunion. There was nothing on the bulletin board — no signs, no banners, not a single word of welcome for the old soldiers. Once there had been letters a foot high on motel marquees in far-flung places from Reno to Nashville — "Welcome World War II Vets," the announcements would read. Or else, "Welcome 124th AAA Gun Battalion." Now, even "Welcome 54th Reunion of the League of Forgotten Men," would have looked good. Better than nothing.

When I checked in, I asked the room clerk where I could find the hospitality suite for the army reunion. She pointed toward a room off the lobby. I decided to go to my room and clean up first. I wanted to be in good shape to meet the old gang and ready for the usual backslapping and jollity that was so much a part of these gatherings.

In its better days, this year's site, with its swimming pool and tennis courts and manicured grounds, had hosted Hollywood people who had come to Scottsdale seeking relaxation. Now the resort was seedy and in need of restoration, its glamour having long ago faded. The place was not crowded, even though the rates were unusually low even for early fall. I noticed several college kids hanging out by the pool, drinking beer and laughing. In the parking lot near the tennis courts there were a few RV rigs, along with a beat-up blue pickup truck with Oklahoma plates. Some elderly people were sitting in the lobby, and among them a few of the men from the old outfit. They were wearing their reunion baseball caps from our meeting two years before.

An hour or so later I walked into the hospitality suite. The atmosphere was restrained. In earlier days, these hospitality suites were the boisterous headquarters for the reunions, where the booze flowed from breakfast until late in the evening, with the noise shattering your ear-drums. The rooms would be crammed with all the old gang, the hillbillies and the ridgerunners and the dirt farmers, drinking, playing cards, and swapping stories. All my "goombas" from the Bay area would be there — Hank Stefani, Pete Sarubi, Ed Soares, George Duranto and Vito Sangervasi. Whiskey, gin and vodka bottles would be lined up on the tables, flanked by oversized buckets of ice filled with bottles of beer. There would be pretzels and potato chips, and the men would be embracing and laughing and telling each other lies — like how well they looked or how they hadn't changed a bit since the old days at Camp Haan, even though most of the men couldn't see the tops of their shoes when they looked down. The late Tommy Hooks, a cook in A Battery during the war, would be stationed behind the wet bar mixing drinks, reenacting his old role of serving the men. But all that was more than twenty years ago, and our gatherings had been gradually going downhill year after year. It wasn't that the men didn't want to attend anymore — it was mainly because they were retired and living on tight budgets, with most of them in poor health and unable to travel. Of course, others, too many others, had by now passed away. After all, we were old men, in our seventies and eighties, the age when each of us hears the sound of the bugler playing taps in the background, the notes seemingly getting louder all the time.

In this year's hospitality suite, there were just a few six packs of Budweiser, nothing else. Some of the old crowd was there, but not enough of them. I saw Arvid Silbert, a lieutenant from B battery. He's a former Chicagoan, now living in retirement in Sarasota. We greeted each other warmly. He, Dick Smith, who was a lieutenant from C battery, and Bowen Smith, a retired colonel and my former battery commander, are the only three officers believed to be living out of the 29 originally assigned to the battalion in 1943.

Ed Soares is a sharp intelligent man whom I have know since, well, it seems like forever. I have a picture of the two of us in front of Mozart's birthplace in Salzburg taken in the summer of 1945 — it is one of my dearest possessions. I keep it on my desk together with a snapshot of the two of us taken close to 50 years later.

I caught a glimpse of Perry Brinegar walking toward me. We shook hands. He's a tall cowboy from Duncan, Oklahoma, who dips snuff and has the perennial brown snuff-dipper's eyeliner rimming his mouth. He offered me a pinch only because he is an inherently polite man, not because he thought I'd take him up on it. I said hello to Ralph and Phyllis Olsen, reunion regulars from Vancouver, Washington. A more amiable couple never lived.

Now I walked over to chat with my old friend, Bruce Brodie. How close we were at one time, and still are. When we were boys of 18 he had been nearly a head taller than I, but hip surgery had whittled off a few inches of his height. We made a date for lunch the following day.

I saw Cortez Hunter drinking beer in a corner of the room. He walked over, and we shook hands. He told me his wife had died, his second wife, and for company he had brought along his first wife and their daughter.

I waved hello to Alvin "Huey" Long, a big jovial Oklahoman, who was this year's reunion chairman. He now lives in Chandler, Arizona. He was with a lady friend whom he introduced as a road buddy, a fellow member of a club called the RV Loners, people who travel the highways without permanent companions. I next caught sight of Don Marks, one of the few bachelors in the battalion. He never misses a reunion. Every year he takes the Greyhound bus from his home in Akron, Ohio, to wherever we're meeting.

I spotted Dee Lemaster and his wife, two salt-of-the-earth people, and reached across the table where they were seated drinking beer, to shake their hands. They're from Amarillo, and if we were to hold a reunion in Timbuctu you could count on their showing up. Same for Frank Fratello who sat clutching a can of beer and scribbling down the names of the players for the following day's golf outing. Frank has been the organizer and patron of our golf tournament for as far back as I can remember. He is more committed than ever to these events even though today the players consist mainly of the relatives of the soldiers. Not many of the men from the battalion are still up to playing 18 holes.

When I asked Don Marks if he was going to sing at the

reunion, he brightened immediately, then nodded and smiled. Don knows most of the songs from the late 30's and 40's, and renders a few during our Saturday night banquets, a cappella. The time has long past when we had a formal program at our banquets, and Don, who in the old days rarely had a chance to get up and perform, has now become a mainstay of the program.

"I have a request for Saturday, Don," I said.

"Just name it. If I know it I'll sing it."

"It's called 'I'm Stepping Out with a Memory Tonight.'"

He looked puzzled for a moment.

"Come on over here," I said, drawing him to a corner of the room. "Let me clue you." And I proceeded to sing the opening of the refrain. "I'm stepping out with a memory tonight/ To paint the town the way we use to do/We'll dine at the old cafe..." And then I said:

"Got it, Don?"

"Yeah, yeah," he replied, and then, the lyrics sinking in, he went on to sing: "...And order cocktails for two instead of the usual one..."

"Attaboy, Don," I said, as I put my arm around him and gave him a hug.

Pretty soon I walked over to the registration table. I had to cough up some money for the banquet, and get my badge. Tony and Kathy Rodrigues, who had handled reservations ever since the reunions began, weren't at their usual posts. Tony was in his room lying down, and his wife, Kathy, was with him. Tony finally had to quit the job which, apart from manning the registration table, entailed getting the mailings out, keeping the mailing list current and of course excising the names of the deceased. It was thankless work, but the two of them handled it efficiently for half a century, uncomplainingly. A few years back, Tony had developed what I'm told was a non-Hodgkins lymphoma, and had grown progressively weaker. But he is a tough soldier and the reunions are his life, and he wasn't going to miss this year's, no matter what. For moral support, the Rodrigues's two daughters and their husbands had come along.

Tina Bruess, the daughter of my friend, Ed Soares, who lives in Phoenix, was filling in for Tony and Kathy. The fee for the banquet and various odds and ends was $36, and after I paid her, she asked:

"Did you see the list?"

She pointed to a lined yellow sheet scotch-taped to the registration table. It was a list of the recently deceased men in the battalion. I scanned the names. I knew about the deaths of some of them, but actually seeing their names on the list served as yet another, even more distressing, reminder of their passing. I looked around the hospitality suite and realized that one day, someone, in some run-down motel in Las Vegas or Denver or Portland, would be looking down at a yellow sheet of paper containing the names of some of the same men who now sat quietly drinking their beers, my own name included. My eyes went down the sheet slowly. I saw Phil Rodriguez's name and Earl White's and Tony Franco's, along with a few others, and some of the wives. Then I came to the last name on the page. It was Captain John Behl from Tulsa. I grabbed the edge of the table. I hadn't heard about John.

"John Behl?" I said to Tina, in shock. "Are you sure about this?"

"Yes," she said, sadly. "He had a massive heart attack in the spring."

"Good Lord!" And then I asked her:

"Is Marilouise here?"

"Yes," she said. "She's staying with Pete Morgan over in Paradise Valley."

"How's she doing?"

"She's okay," Tina said.

"This is really a tough one," I said.

"I know," she said, nodding.

"And then there were three," I said.

"What?"

"Nothing, Tina, just thinking out loud."

Pete Morgan is a nephew of Marilouise's, a former army major who collects and sells war memorabilia, including memorabilia from the 124th. Whenever our conclaves are held in Phoenix, Pete and his wife put on a magnificent party in our honor.

John Behl was my friend, a friend of Jews, a man who had worked for Jews in Muskogee and Okmulgee. I thought about the time, a few years before, at our 52nd reunion, when John and Marilouise had dined with my wife and me at the Erie Cafe in Chicago. He had ordered calves liver the moment he saw it on the menu. There was no deliberation, and when he had cleaned his plate he let out a contented groan and pronounced it the best meal he had ever eaten. He never stopped talking about that liver all through the weekend. The following year, when the battalion met in Las Vegas, John was still consumed by the memory of the calves liver in Chicago. How that man loved liver.

Tina Bruess is a conscientious, warm hearted young woman. Her father, Ed, is a Portuguese from Hayward, California, a sharp, intelligent man whom I have known since — well, it seems like forever. I have a picture of the two us standing very erect in front of Mozart's birthplace in Salzburg, taken in the summer of 1945, shortly after the war ended. A few years ago, Ed sent me the picture, which he had enlarged and framed. It is one of my dearest possessions. I keep it on a desk in my study, together with a snapshot of the two us, in somewhat the same pose, taken close to fifty years later.

The first time I saw Ed he had a handlebar moustache, the kind so many of the British soldiers had. It was full-bodied and twirled on the ends, and it gave him so much dash that I tried to affect the same moustache myself. He still has his today, although the growth is less luxuriant than it once was. My own was so puny that I got rid of it before I came home from Europe.

Ed is one of the few men who has kept our annual meetings going. He and a few others got the reunions started back in 1949, a mere three years after we were discharged, and from then on Ed appointed himself as our leader and "president." Make no mistake, he is the man in charge. He has run things all through the years, and his will usually prevails. The men are his sheep, and I'm the first to admit that I'm one of them. The explanation for Ed's power is that no one else wants to do anything except come to the gatherings and enjoy themselves. Lately, however, it seems that the men come together annually less for having a good time and more for the simple reassurance of being together. Ed still tackles all the dirty work, and the service he has performed over the years can't be minimized.

I asked Tina about her mother, Alma, who is a cancer patient. Tina told me that her mother had insisted on attending the reunion even though she was hardly in any condition to make the trip. When I saw Alma that evening, she was full of energy and had a bright hopeful attitude. She told me she felt better than she had in weeks. But her body, all 86 pounds of it, was conveying another story.

I sat around with some of the group in the hospitality suite and talked for a while, but I grew weary very soon. I wanted to be by myself. Seeing the names on that yellow sheet had drained me. I grabbed a can of beer and strolled out toward the swimming pool. It had cooled down a bit. The college kids were gone, and I sat down on a lounge chair to watch what was left of the sunset.

I couldn't help thinking about all the men who had passed away since the war ended. I can remember their faces but not all of their names. The 124th AAA Gun Battalion was 750 men strong when we were activated in 1943 at Camp Haan, California. Now there were fewer than 200 names left on Tony Rodrigues's mailing list, but nobody knows how many of those were still alive. Only thirty men had shown up in Scottsdale, most of them no strangers to heart ailments, diabetes, cancer and Parkinson's disease. My old friends, Danny Cicchelli, Herman Reading, Earl White, Phil Rodriguez and John Behl — all were gone, and so were many others with whom I had grown old. I mourn for all of them, and most especially, for Joe Snopek, my old A Battery top-kick, a man who had a profound influence on my life. Joe Snopek. It is during moments like these, when I reflect on the life and near-death of the old battalion, that I think about Joe and how he tried, not altogether successfully, to make a man out of me.

TWO

The first time I saw Joe was late in the spring of 1943. I had just finished my basic training at Camp Callan, near LaJolla, California, where we recruits, for all our ineptitude, were treated like members of the privileged class. Was this the army, the United States Army, molder of men? I could hardly believe it. Meeting Joe was a rude awakening. In all my eighteen years I had never come across anyone as tough on me as Joe had been. He was first sergeant of A Battery, part of the original cadre of the battalion, then a newly activated unit where I had been assigned as a 636 Intelligence Observer, a fancy term the army used for forward scouts and artillery observers. To this day, I'm not entirely sure why Joe had it in for me, but almost from the beginning his dislike for me was evident to everyone within earshot of his voice.

On my first day at Camp Haan, I had left the latrine on my way back to my barracks when I heard his voice. It ripped through me as sharply as a chain saw felling trees.

"Hey, you, didja see all that shit you walked over. Clean it up, all of it. Every stinkin' cigarette butt and banana husk in the goddamn area. Get it out of my sight, now."

I turned to face the voice, my legs trembling, and there he stood, a hulking figure with five stripes on his sleeve, three over two, diamond in the center. That voice was one I came to know painfully for the next fourteen months in the states. It never lost its angry tone, and rarely did I hear that snarl directed to anyone but me. Once we arrived overseas, Joe stopped riding me. By that time, it was too late. There was nothing more he could do for me.

Camp Callan was not really a proper training ground for the real army, Joe Snopek's kind of army. Callan was a newly constructed army camp, a few miles from LaJolla, then a sedate little community with flowers in bloom everywhere. Our treatment there seemed to have been influenced by our surroundings. The non-coms never raised their voices or pushed us too hard. Why that was is still a mystery. Maybe they felt that loud noises would wilt the flowers. In any event, I was barely aware a war was going on.

It was a different matter when I got to Camp Haan, a mere sixty or so miles to the east in Riverside. It was a dusty, scruff-filled encampment on the edge of the Mojave desert. There were grim reminders of war everywhere — from our big 90-millimeter guns to the roar of the B-24's coming from March Field, across the highway. Our training regimen had become more rigorous, and discipline had tightened to a point where I was suffocating from it. It was here that Joe Snopek was the reigning tyrant, a man more powerful than many of the officers, his voice more fearful, his bearing more menacing.

Joe rode me unmercifully. I know for a fact that I pulled more KP than any man in the battery with the exception of my pal, Danny Cicchelli. But why? There was something about me, I suppose, something that made Joe peg me as a screw-off right from the beginning. I have no idea exactly what. That discovery will probably have to wait until I write my biography — hear me right, not my autobiography. I'm talking about an undertaking requiring a scrupulously independent viewpoint. Maybe I would even disguise myself. It would be hard to pull off but I'd talk to some of the people who knew me back then, well over a half-century ago. I'd ask them what they thought of that scrawny kid from Iowa, not letting on that it was I asking the questions. Don't hold back, I'd tell them, because this is going to be the most definitive, even-handed biography ever written. No holds barred. Strictly objective.

The only trouble with that idea is that there aren't many people alive to talk with, including most of the men I served with in the army. So you'll have to take my word for one thing: Joe definitely had his mind made up about me from the start. Sensing this, it was natural for me to figure that anything I did to redeem myself wouldn't make any difference anyway, so I continued to screw off. It wasn't that goldbricking didn't come naturally for me, or that I could have changed — it was mainly a matter of my not even trying to mend my ways.

Furthermore, since Joe had access to my file, he probably figured that there was justification for the way he treated me. Maybe he subscribed to the long-standing myth that Jews try hard to avoid combat service and instead manage to get assigned to the Quartermaster Corps or other non-combat units, I merely being the oddball exception. There was also the fact that A battery had 147 men, among whom I was the only Jew, and that the battalion as a whole, its headquarters battery and all four of its 90-millimeter gun batteries and 750 men, still had only one Jew — me. With

Camp Callan was not really a proper training ground for the real army, Joe Snopek's kind of army. Callan was a newly constructed army camp, a few miles from La Jolla, then a sedate little community with flowers in bloom everywhere.

regard to the myth itself, some of the men who had hurled anti-Semitic comments my way during the war, and, yes, even long after it had ended, evidently hadn't known Al Peskin or Sid Pruce, two friends I had gone to Hebrew school with in Des Moines, whose brief army careers as infantrymen ended abruptly on the battle-fields in the South Pacific in 1943. I doubt too whether the per-petrators of the myth paid attention to all the Stars of David on grave markers at the military cemetery at St. Mere Eglise, a bloody little town where we bivouaced after the Normandy invasion in 1944. The cemetery hadn't reached its capacity then and hadn't yet been prettied up as it is today, but even a glance at it would provide a strong moral lesson — that only when Jew and gentile were mortally wounded and lying side by side, would the myth of the non-combatant Jew be confronted.

Nevertheless, for all of Joe's abuse, no matter what inspired it, he was a good human being. As I think about him today, I believe he saw me for what I was, a spoiled punk of a kid, Jew, gen-tile or whatever, who needed to become a man, and he took what steps he deemed necessary to make me one.

The last time I saw Joe was at the Maxim Hotel in Las Vegas where we were holding our 42nd reunion. He was no longer that gruff, bull-necked brute of a man I first came across at Camp Haan in 1943. Back then he had a short neck, massive shoulders, and biceps large enough to pop the stitching off his stripes. But this 1985 fellow wasn't the Joe Snopek I remembered. This one was visibly sick and very thin, almost unrecognizably so.

I had lost my fear of Joe during our long months in combat and in the ensuing years, and now, as I looked at him, I could feel only an unbearable sadness.

"Hey, Sarge," I said, cheerily, as I approached him, my hand extended. "It's been a long time."

For a moment, he seemed not to recognize me, but then a glint of recognition crossed his face. Finally, it dawned on him.

"Marks, aw, Marks, for Chris'sake," he cried out. "I didn't know you were coming."

He was glad to see me, and yet sad, too. I thought I saw his eyes cloud up. I wanted to embrace him, and I think he felt the same way, but we each hesitated. Instead I grabbed his hand in a grip of friendship, and grasped his forearm with my other hand.

"It's good to see you, Joe," I said, "real good."

"I'll be damned, I'll be damned. It's my "favorite martian.""

"The very same."

"Are you still screwing off ?" he asked, breaking into a smile.

"Only when you're not around to straighten me out, Joe," I said.

He smiled again, no doubt thinking of the old days at Camp Haan and the role he played in making a soldier out of me. I know he sensed that I was thinking the same thing. We chatted a while about our lives since the war ended, and he told me that he had gotten sick about two years before. It hadn't been easy for him getting to Las Vegas from St. Louis, but he wanted desperately to see the old gang. In fact, he had to arrange for his dialysis treatments at a Vegas hospital before leaving St. Louis. I was sure he knew that this was to be his last reunion. All of us realized it, too. We only had to take a look at him. Good old Joe. He had made army life hell for me, and I for him.

From reunion to reunion, from hotel to hotel, from one coast to the other, the voices of my comrades, living and dead, still echo through the banquet halls and ballrooms of my memory. The ranks are thinning down to bare bones but we continue to meet. Nowadays, the widows often are taking the places of their dead husbands. If they weren't around to bolster the attendance, our reunions could be held on someone's back porch. As these things will happen, the wives who attend with their husbands (as most of them do) have become as bound to one another as the men.

Seldom in our country's history, I'm quite sure, has any battalion, offically disbanded by the war department over fifty years before, so vigorously refused to be broken up. I don't know what all the reasons are but I think many of us feel that if the battalion survives, we, even as a dwindling group of has-beens, somehow might survive, too. There is no other army unit like ours, no other one which holds a reunion every single year, no other one in which the men cling so desperately to one another, no other one that, I'm told, has a pistol stashed away for the last survivor to use instead of having to face the next reunion alone.

The gatherings started spontaneously back in 1949, a little more than three years after we were discharged. Some of the California boys had gotten together for informal conclaves on their own. But by the early 1950's they had expanded to include everybody. These annual events came to be like beacons in the night to all of us. We would drop what we were doing and come running, following the call of our buddies to places like Panorama City, Reno, Indianapolis, St. Louis, Chicago, Nashville, Reno, Phoenix and Las Vegas. One letter from Ed Soares was all it took. Some of the sentimentalists like myself needed no prodding, others required a bit of urging from our battalion social director and tracer of lost persons, the late Ed Harris, a man who spent his vacations tracking down and visiting men from the battalion.

I think back. It is December, 1945. I am agog with joy. Along with most of the men, I am in Marseilles, at Camp Lucky Strike, waiting to board a Liberty Ship for home. I am sick of being with them, and I feel they must be just as sick of being with me. Most of us have been together for three gruelling years, through our training days in the states and our combat time overseas. I don't say goodbye to anyone. No handshakes, no see-ya-laters. I'm out of it; that's all that matters. I met them at 18, now I'm nearly 22. We were strangers when we met. I look at them now and they are still strangers. They speak in funny accents and come from strange places, and most of them have never knowingly laid eyes on a Jew, and have no conception of what one looks like. All they know is that they don't like them. That's one fact that's been made very clear to me. But all that's over, and now I'm going home to Chicago. HOME BY CHRISTMAS. HOME BY CHRISTMAS. That's what the guys are saying. But where is home? Chicago? I'll have to think about that. My mother is there but that's the only connection I have. Des Moines, where I grew up and have friends, is behind me, and I have no desire to go back to live with my relatives, my mother's family, where for too many years I had been the resident orphan. I shudder when I think about it. Home, like it or not, is with my mother, no escaping it. Before the army, there had been Wichita, Des Moines, Phoenix, Lansing, Chicago. Before the army, I had never been out of her sight.

I grew up surrounded by women — great aunts, aunts, cousins, and a mother who made me the center of her universe. I was three years old when my parents divorced, and I never again saw my father. That was in 1927 when divorces were unthinkable for Jews. My mother never re-married; it would have been better for all concerned — her brothers and sisters, her various relatives at large, but especially for me — had she done so. Most likely she had made a conscious decision to go it alone, preferring to make me her child-husband and gentleman-in-waiting, a status imposed upon me at the tender age of three that finally was snatched away from me by the army. If all of those who suffered hideous losses and untold sorrow from World War II can forgive me for saying it, I would like to declare that the war, that big wonderful, exciting war, instead of taking my life, had actually saved it. But only for a while.

I am aboard the SS Thomas Wolfe. They talk about the trip home taking 17 days, 17 days to nowhere. My mother has little money, and she and I will go back to a life in one room apartments, just as it had been when I was drafted. Three years earlier, if the doctors at the induction center could have seen inside my head I probably would have been classified 4-F. What would they classify me now, now on my way back to a life with my mother in one-room apartments.

I seem to have grown up without any vision of my future. After I was discharged from the army, I had no specific goals, no burning desire to do much of anything. I didn't even have a high school diploma, and didn't really care whether I ever had one or not. But the principal of Senn High School in Chicago, where I had been a senior in the class of 1942, sent me an honorary diploma after my army discharge in 1946. It showed me to be a graduate of the class of 1946, four years too late — a sheet of parchment eight years and four high schools in the making. Keep in mind that all manner of men have received honorary doctors' degrees from hundreds of universities. They're handed out like toys in a box of Cracker Jacks. My diploma, on the other hand, an honorary high school degree, is far more rare.

Not being entirely without purpose in life, I found myself heading for Bonds, a clothing store on State street in Chicago, shortly after my discharge. I was wearing my uniform. I had several hundred dollars of savings and separation pay in my pocket along with a heart full of hope, more hope than either education or experience. The years under the thumb of Joe Snopek were swept from my mind like crumbs from the dinner table, and I was off to Bonds to get a new start in life and a new suit of clothes to match. I wanted to dress like my father, the man in the photograph I carried around. He was a real sharpie, so the photos revealed, from his snap-brim fedoras to his tightly-knotted four-in-hand ties to his soft-shouldered suits.

I purchased a powder-blue, chalk-striped suit, a one-button Picadilly Roll, as the salesman described it. It was a suit that only a gentleman like me would wear, the salesman said. The lapels flowed in a long graceful arc down to a point just off to the side of my crotch where they merged into a single button. My father, even in the throes of his wildest gambling escapades, would never have worn a suit like that. I have a snapshot of myself, taken by my Aunt Bessie in her driveway in Des Moines. As I look at it today and see that skinny kid with a pile of curly hair, wearing that outlandish suit, I want to cry out in shame.

My mother and I had moved to Chicago from Phoenix in 1941, several months before Pearl Harbor, after a short stopover with relatives in Des Moines. That was the year my father died, alone and penniless in a hospital in Ottawa, Kansas. His body was crushed by a speeding locomotive, his 1939 Plymouth, behind in payments to the dealer, was as crushed as he was. But neither the body nor the car were as devastated in spirit as my father must have been. I travelled to Ottawa with my mother to claim the body. We checked into one of those walk-up-one-flight hotels on the main street and got the least expensive room. It had no bath and only one bed, and I spent that night in the same bed with my mother. The next morning I went to the funeral home to see my father's body but was denied admittance. I had not seen him since I was a toddler, and I retain only two images of him — one chewing on a cigar, his lips, when he kissed me, wet from tobacco juice; the other, lugging his salesman's sample cases into our third floor apartment in Wichita. A year and a half after my father died, I would be in the army. He left me his Masonic ring — there were holes where the diamond chips had been removed. It was all he could call his own.

I went to college after the army, courtesy of the G.I. Bill. I found a job in 1950, and got married the same year. My wife and I had children, and later on grandchildren — the saga of Mr. Everyman told in fewer than twenty-five words. Later on, during my retirement, thoughts of my days in the army suddenly came bursting out of their hiding place. The army was something I could point to with pride, a means of countering self-devaluation, that nitwitted hallmark of retirement that often sets in with old age.

These days I carry a clipboard in my head. On it are the names of all the surviving men of the battalion. Quite often I have a powerful urge to phone them, especially the ones who are ill, to make sure they're still alive. Once I put a mental check mark next to their names, knowing that they're all present and accounted for, I'm okay, at least for a while, or until the next wave of concern comes along. So when I learn that I'll never be able to make that mental check mark alongside a buddy's name, my grief is painful. The news chips off a piece of my own life as well as a piece of the lives of my buddies. Officially, you see, there is no battalion any more. We're just a memory, nothing more than a piece of dusty paper in a war department file. Too many more chips and there won't even be that.

When a regular reunion-goer doesn't show up, no one says much about it, but the missing buddy is cause for a great deal of alarm. The suspense can be unbearable until finally someone musters the courage to find out why. When the report comes back that "old Vito couldn't afford to make the trip this year..." — well, that would be the good news.

Understand, please, that we were destined to remain together for our lifetimes, no matter what we felt about one another back at Camp Lucky Strike. We may have only seemed unshackled for a time after the war, but separation from one another has promised only emptiness. You don't separate yourself from your siblings. You don't break up families or cut the bonds of friendship, warend or no war-end.

That is why we had gathered in Las Vegas that day. We sat quietly as Joe Snopek got up to say a few words at our Saturday night banquet, the final event of our three-day bash. As he stood before us, a frail apparition, he struggled to hold back his tears. He said his one wish was to have the insignia of the 124th on his casket when he died. He told us how much we meant to him, we who

Understand, please, that we were destined to remain together for our lifetimes, no matter what we felt about one another back at Camp Lucky Strike. We may have only seemed unshackled for a time after the war, but separation from one another has promised only emptiness.

would always be "my men." That's what he called us, "my men." Yes, Joe, we are your men, and probably always will be. If you didn't know it when you were alive, know it now, know it forever, as your body lies beneath the insignia of the 124th. We are your men, Joe, no matter how miserable you once made our lives.

That night, the big banquet room in Las Vegas was crowded with over-the-hill warriors. As Joe spoke, I noticed that I wasn't the only one whose eyes were moist. I knew all of them would always consider themselves "Joe's men," just as I still do. I hated myself for thinking about it at the time but I remembered the night at Camp Haan in 1943 when Elvin Hardin and I extracted our revenge on Joe. Joe had stepped outside of A Battery headquarters and, seeing us walking down the hill toward the PX, asked us to do him a favor. Would we bring him back a ham sandwich? Yeah, sure, Sarge, sure thing. We did as he asked, but on our way back Elvin grabbed my arm and steered me toward the latrine.

"What's going on," I asked.

"Watch, you'll see. We'll get that sonofabitch."

Once inside the latrine, Elvin carefully unwrapped Joe's ham sandwich and unbuttoned his pants. Then he took out his penis and rubbed it around on the ham, first on one side of the sandwich then on the other. When he was finished he broke into a big laugh. He asked me if I would like a turn. For a moment I was tempted but shook my head. Somehow, the circumsized penis of a Jew rubbed over *traife* meat would be more of a punishment to the perpetrator than to the victim. Elvin shrugged, then carefully rewrapped the sandwich and we trudged up the hill to present it to Joe, stifling a laugh as we handed it to him.

Elvin was a lanky leather-faced kid from Texas with a perpetually sun-tanned face. When he spoke it was like listening to a bit-player in a western movie. Apart from physical appearances, Elvin was not one of us. The rumor had gotten around that he had a high score on his Army General Classification Test (the army's version of an IQ test.) A score of 110 was required to become an officer; Elvin had 145. One day, without fanfare, without anyone even noticing, Elvin was gone, evaporating like a puff of smoke. Where he went, and where he is today, no one seems to know. No one seems to care, except me. I think about him everytime I bite into a ham sandwich, wondering if by chance he had gotten to that particular sandwich ahead of me.

It was with a mixture of love and regret that I recalled that incident. I hated myself for having been so young and stupid and for thinking about it now at such a sad moment while Joe was making his farewell speech.

The only time I became really angry with Joe was in the fall of 1943 while we were still at Camp Haan. It was during morning inspection. Joe suddenly barked out: "All Jews fall out." I remember that I alone broke ranks while the rest of the battery was dismissed. What the hell was going on? Joe approached me and pushed his face into mine, his jaw jutting forward.

"I don't know what kind of an army we're running," he snorted, each syllable etched in anger, "but you've got a three day pass for the Jewish holidays, Marks, so make sure you spend the time praying. You're sure as hell going to need it when you get back."

I was stunned. I could hardly believe my good luck. Three precious days in L.A. Instantly I began reviewing all my entertainment options — the bars on Hollywood Boulevard, filled with lonely women, the Hollywood canteen, and best of all a date with Anita whose telephone number a friend in Chicago had given me. Her name was Anita Durchin, and she lived with her parents on Cochran street in the Fairfax district. I called her and arranged to meet her just as soon as I got a pass to L.A. Her voice on the phone had been lovely, sweet and welcoming. Now, thanks to Joe Snopek, I was finally going to meet her. I began to sing Johnny "Scat" Davis's rendition of "Hooray For Hollywood." As for attending Jewish services while I was in L.A.— that was the most unlikely option of all.

Anita, as it turned out, was older and more sophisticated than I, and more beautiful than I dared to hope. Sensing my loneliness, she wrote to me regularly throughout Europe. Her letters, which fell just short of the kind of promises of love I sought, sustained me through the war. Despite the fact that I had not spent more than a few hours with her a long, long time ago, I have never stopped thinking about her, and have never stopped searching for her.

I have Joe to thank for all of that. It wasn't his idea to send me to L.A., of course, but it was his gruff command that made it happen and enabled me to meet Anita. How do you thank someone who gives you several sublime hours with a lovely woman, a woman you can never forget.

That weekend was when I learned that all women are not innocent and sweet. The lesson came the first night of Rosh Hashonah, the Jewish New Year. Some lesson to learn on the high holidays! I was in a bar on Hollywood Boulevard. I was in Mecca. The lights on the roof of the Roosevelt Hotel glowed in the sky; the Brown Derby was around the corner; Graumman's Chinese Theater was just down the block. I was young and eager. I was sitting in the center of the universe with money in my pocket. The following night I was going to see Anita. As I sat there, contemplating my good fortune, I spotted a girl sitting at the bar. She was alone, and occasionally she would look over in my direction. She was young and attractive and very shapely. She had the face of a cherub, framed with blonde curls. She looked like a grown up, sexy Shirley Temple. I bought her one drink, then another, then two more, matching her drink for drink. I was spending my money wildly. I took her to some joint for dinner where we had more drinks. She began leaning against me, rubbing my thigh, kissing my ear, and I was sure that at last I was going to get lucky. The more it seemed like a sure thing, the more my legs shook in excitement. But where would we go? She lived with her parents, and I was staying at the Lutheran USO on Ivar street. No hope in either place.

"I have an idea," she said. "How about the beach at Santa Monica?"

I had no idea where Santa Monica was.

"Okay with me," I said, trying not to sound too eager. "But how do we get there?"

"Don't you have a car?"

I shook my head. Hell, I didn't even have a driver's license.

She thought for a moment, then slapped the table. She was beaming.

"How about hitch-hiking there," she said.

"What?"

"Yeah, we'll thumb a ride." She waved her thumb and lifted her skirt slightly. "You know, like in the movie."

"It Happened One Night," I reminded her.

"What?"

"The movie, the movie you're talking about, *It Happened One Night*. Claudette Colbert lifts up her skirt and, whoa!, a car screeches to a stop."

"Yeah," she said, blankly.

I rose from the table and took her arm.

"Let's go," I said. "You lead the way."

"Wait," she said, grabbing my arm. "We can't hitch-hike together."

"Why not?"

"Because cars won't stop for two people."

"I see," I said, confused. "Well, how do I get there? How do you get there?"

My questions were making her impatient.

"Look, here's what I want you to do," she said, speaking very slowly. "I want you to hitch-hike across Highland to Santa Monica Boulevard. When you get there be standing on the northwest corner. Highland runs north and south, this way."

As she spoke she drew an imaginary diagram on the table-cloth with her finger.

"Okay," I said, "then what do I do?"

"Don't do anything," she explained, "just wait for me. I'll catch a ride farther east on Santa Monica, then when I see you I'll tell the driver to stop, and we'll ride out to the beach together."

"But what if the driver doesn't stop?"

"Don't worry. He'll stop. I'll tell him it's his patriotic duty. Honestly, you worry too much. It's going to be fine." She placed her hand on my knee and ran it up my thigh, then she leaned over and kissed me.

I paid the check and we walked out of the restaurant together. I had blown half of my money, but at that moment I didn't care. We kissed again as we stood on the sidewalk, the lights of Hollywood Boulevard brilliant in the warm September night. I held her close. I was 18 years old. She was several years older. My legs were trembling uncontrollably. I began singing under my breath.

Hooray for Hollywood,
You screwy ballyhooey Hollywood

"I can't wait, my sweetheart," she said.

"Neither can I," I whispered, my voice hoarse.

I got a ride to Highland and Santa Monica. It was easy. I immediately took up my position on the northwest corner, and waited for her. And waited, and waited, all the time thinking about my coming baptism of fire, my first time with a woman, the consecration to take place here in the City of Lost Angels, as the writer John Fante called it, on this the highest of Jewish holy days.

But where was she? There was no sign of her. I was growing impatient. I had been standing on the corner for over half an hour, and I was beginning to have misgivings. I put them out of my mind immediately. Maybe it was simply a case of her not being able to get a ride. It couldn't be anything else. I was sure she was just as eager as I was. Another ten minutes went by before I saw her. She was sitting on the ledge of the back seat of a convertible, waving and laughing. The driver, a civilian, was honking his horn, and he was laughing, too. There were a couple of other passengers, a man and a woman, both young and also laughing. The horn kept blaring as their car passed me, disappearing in the blur of lights on the boulevard.

I stood there in a daze, not willing to believe what had happened. Then I started to think of all the money I'd spent. I had planned to spend most of it on my date with Anita the next night. I was overcome with self-loathing for having been taken and for blowing all that money. But then came the worst thought of all. I thought about my mother back in Chicago. I had phoned her and told her I was going to L.A. to attend Rosh Hashonah services. I knew that would please her. I also asked her to wire me some money. She sent me forty dollars, money she had worked hard for as a clerk at the Bureau of Public Debt. That kind of money was a fortune — money for a new dress or for something to brighten up the one-room apartment we shared. It was a major sacrifice, blood sucked out of her veins, marrow extracted from her bones, and for what — so that her lying, no-account son could turn it over to some whore. Oh dear God, I was just like my father, a man with the same no-account ways. It was God's way of punishing me for not attending Rosh Hashonah services. I was sure of it. Worst of all, I had sold my heritage down the river for a *shiksa*, the arch-enemy of all good Jewish boys, the arch-rival of all Jewish mothers, especially single Jewish mothers. Like mine.

I continued standing on the corner. It was growing late. I had nowhere to go except back to the USO. Idly, I began singing, each word sticking in my throat,

> Hooray for Hollywood
> You screwy, ballyhooey Hollywood
> Where any young mechanic
> Can be a panic...

until the song finally died on my lips.

Before the morning that I was singled out as a Jew, I had no inkling if anyone knew I was Jewish or not, and I didn't think much about it. After Joe's abrupt announcement, however, I became known as "The Jew." To most of the men I was "Marks," but to a few others I was simply "The Jew." That three-day pass, to this day, has not been forgotten. It has been an issue for well over half a century. I am reminded of it at every reunion. What is most vexing to my buddies is not the three day pass alone but the fact that I didn't have to make restitution by spending the

Christmas holiday in camp. Joe's ham-handed handling of things had made me a target of ridicule all these years.

We had a cocktail party at Pete Morgan's home during our 51st reunion in Phoenix. It was in honor of our battalion, and most of the men and their wives were there. In addition, there were several guests, friends and neighbors of the host and hostess. It was a lovely party, the atmosphere refined and subdued. I was rather surprised at how civil and well-behaved my comrades were. They had come a long way since our army days when they were fresh off the truck farms of Texas and California. I remember standing in the living room chatting with an attractive stylishly dressed woman when the words of one of the men thundered through the room.

"Hey, Jew," he said, walking toward me.

I looked at my companion. I was red faced and embarrassed. I smiled weakly at my buddy, barely acknowledging his greeting. My companion, however, was not smiling. Thank heaven for that.

She and I had dinner together later that evening. As we were finishing our coffee, she confronted me about my comrade's remark.

"That was a terrible thing he said to you. What an awful person."

"He's really not a bad guy," I assured her. "We've known each other for over 50 years."

"Fifty years or 100 years, it makes no difference. He's still an awful person."

My companion was a gentile, and I was heartened by the outrage she felt, but embarrassed that I hadn't responded angrily to the remark. I would have, I knew, had it been anyone else. The fact is I have never confronted any of the men about their anti-Semitic comments. I'm not sure why. Maybe it's so important to me to be a part of the group and a member in good standing that I'm willing to accept any old slur that comes my way. As I've said, the 124th is my family, and you don't separate yourself from your siblings, no matter what.

THREE

My army baptism took place in February, 1943, at Camp Grant, Illinois. My army serial number was 36742228. I have never forgotten it, and never will forget it. It is burned into my memory like the brand on the rump of a steer. It was stamped on the dog tags which hung around my neck through five training camps in the states and through five war torn countries.

I lost my original dog tags a long time ago, but a few years back when I was having one of my periodic feelings of nostalgia about the army, I had duplicates made. The color of the metal is wrong, and they aren't stamped with an "H" (for Hebrew), and they don't have notches on the ends to wedge between your jaws when the burial detail comes along to scoop up your bones. Without those notches, imagine all the confusion when you're buried under someone else's grave marker and the Stars of David get mixed up with the crosses.

Our journey into war began, as I have said, at Camp Callan, California, where most of us took our basic training. We were then the 52nd AA Training Battalion. LaJolla was then a quiet, genteel community of white haired, beautifully dressed retirees strolling unhurriedly along the palm-lined streets or sitting on the veranda of the Valencia Hotel, the shops elegant and the clerks smiling and composed. We soldiers from Camp Callan were the only jarring note, unpleasant reminders in khaki that somewhere out there a war was in progress and that four miles away boys were being readied for slaughter like chickens in a federally supervised poultry plant.

Today, it would be hard to imagine that there had once been an army camp on that site; or that the camp had once sprawled over what are now the rolling green fairways of Torrey Pines golf course; or that my barracks, in fact, had stood only an easy 5-iron shot away from the 12th green. Today, millionaire golf pros cooly stride the fairways where a lifetime ago young kids in boots ran obstacle courses and at night tearfully wrote letters home.

Camp Callan had been my first taste of the state of California. It was the beginning of a love affair with the state that's gone on for over a half-century, and I've never been able to explain how it happened. I only know that from the first time I set foot on its soil, maybe even before that, it had cast its spell over me, and I'm still under it. Some romances are like that. They come out of nowhere and last forever. You may marry someone else but you never get over that first love. She may get old and fat and her personality may change for the worse, but what difference does it make? You remember her as she used to be, young, sweet and glamorous, and nothing will open your eyes to the present, so powerful is her hold on you.

Now that I think about it I believe the romance started to take form when I was 12. I was taking dramatic art lessons from Sylpha Snook at the Jewish Community Center in Des Moines and doing impersonations of Maurice Chevalier, Al Jolson and Ted Lewis from the stage of the center's auditorium. I think I was one of Sylpha's favorites because when radio station WHO in Des Moines was airing Sunday afternoon radio dramas from its studio, Sylpha chose me to play the part of a young teen-ager. That was thrill enough but nothing compared to also having "Dutch" Reagan, one of the studio announcers, in the cast. He was then a minor celebrity in Des Moines because he was broadcasting from the WHO studio ticker tapes of the Chicago Cubs' games from Wrigley field. As I remember him then, he was a handsome, athletic-looking fellow but hardly the matinee-idol type. He wore his hair on the short side, parted close to the middle. I have the impression that he wore rimless glasses with hexagonal shaped lenses. His politics, I'm told, were liberal then, but his appearance was strictly midwest conservative.

I was a bit disappointed on the day of the broadcast because "Dutch" read his lines from one studio while I and the rest of the cast members performed in front of two floor microphones in another. I never held that against him, though. He was my hero, my box seat ticket to Wrigley field, supplying me not only with the play-by-play action but all the color as well, even including the taste of hot dogs and pop. The tapes he read from may have sputtered out only a terse transmission, like "Ball two," but as Reagan reported the action, it became..."Klein rubs his hands in the dirt and steps up to the plate. Mungo glances toward first, takes his long slow windup, here comes the pitch...Klein takes a fast ball just over the letters. Ball two on the batter." And so it went through the full nine innings. That colorful, confiding manner of his announcing days carried over to his presidency. As I watched him addressing the nation on TV I would close my eyes and I swear I could hear Dutch calling the balls and strikes from the WHO studios.

It came as quite a blow when he left Des Moines for Hollywood. He was preceded there by the actress Joy Page, a Des Moines gal, who had arranged a screen test for him, or so I was told at the time, and that for me was the end of the greatest part of the game of baseball, listening to the man who would become our president bringing a romance to the game that I wish still existed. I was living in Phoenix when his first movie was released. I saw it at least five times. It was titled *Love is on the Air* and starred Dutch and the beautiful June Travis who, by an odd coincidence, was the daughter of the late Harry Grabiner, general manager of the Chicago White Sox.

I seldom agreed with Reagan's politics but I've always admired him. He was my connection to baseball as I was growing up, and ever since he left for Hollywood he was my connection to that magical boulevard which I believed was paved with gold.

My mother and I moved to Phoenix in 1937 on money she had scraped up from my aunt Bessie and her two younger brothers. I slept on small screened-in balconies, first at our one-room apartment at 1508 North Central and later in another one room flat at 549 West Latham. At night I listened to remote broadcasts of orchestras from Los Angeles nightclubs. I remember the voices of the announcers: — "the music of Henry King coming to you direct from the beautiful Victor Hugo's restaurant." Or "Matty Malneck and his Violin coming to you from the internationally famous Cocoanut Grove on beautiful Wilshire Boulevard," and at that point you could hear the strains of Malneck's signature number, "Stairway to the Stars." — all of it calculated to send a young boy's heart into romantic tailspins. By now the seeds were planted. Those wonderful watering holes are gone, and I have no idea what became of Henry King and Matty Malneck, but now just to remember them is to become caught in a maze of sweet memories.

On our first date, I took Anita to another famous watering hole, called Tail O' the Cock. It was the second night of my memorable Rosh Hashonah weekend. I have no idea how I got wind of the place or how I had enough money to go there after my crazy evening with Shirley Temple, but, ah, the night was wonderful. There I was, dining on LaCienega Boulevard, where the stars dined, and I was with Anita, a beautiful blond-haired Jewish girl. And furthermore, for all I knew, I could have been mistaken for a child actor, lately drafted into the army. I remember drinking a concoction made famous at the restaurant. It was called a Moscow Mule, a mixture of bouillon soup and vodka. I couldn't bear to drink one now, but just to think about it brings back thoughts of Anita, and of Joe Snopek, the man who made it all possible.

My army life began one cold February morning early in 1943. I boarded a train from Union Station in Chicago on my way to Camp Grant, Illinois, a regional induction center 90 miles west of Chicago. My mother had come to see me off just as she had done on my first day of kindergarten in Des Moines. I remember how I kept looking over my shoulder afraid that some of my fellow inductees might see me. I was eighteen, and it would be the first time I would be away from my mother since I was eleven and had spent an unhappy week at Camp Matigwa, a Boy Scout camp near

Boone, Iowa. On second thought, it wasn't even a week. I remember being so terrified of camp life that they had sent me home after five days.

Our processing at Camp Grant completed, we boarded a troop train bound for Camp Callan. It was on the train that I first met Bruce Brodie, a tall raw-boned kid my age from central Michigan. We were assigned to the same compartment, located at the farthest end of one of the sleeping cars. A corporal from the transportation corps was in charge of the entire car, and shared our compartment. He was a pleasant enough fellow, perhaps 10 years older than Bruce and I. During our first evening on board, we had to decide what our sleeping arrangements would be. The compartment had a lower and an upper berth. The corporal and I shared the lower. I doubt whether that kind of intimacy would prevail in today's army, but it was 1943, and wartime expediency was more important than conventional sleeping arrangements.

There was plenty of room for two in the lower. Because the corporal and I were both slim, there was even enough room to allow for kicking and squirming. In the middle of the night, however, I awakened to find the corporal's arms around my waist, his body against mine. He was sound asleep. I tried to ease out of his grasp, but he had me in a Greco-Roman body grip. If a referee had

Bruce Brodie (right) and Bowen Smith. "It was on the troop train bound for Camp Callan that I first met Bruce Brodie, a tall raw-boned kid from Michigan...and we've been friends ever since."

been present he would have slapped the mat three times signifying a fall, but not this night. The corporal would not relinquish his grip. I lay there in terror, not knowing exactly what to do. I could have given him a sharp jab in his ribs, but that seemed risky. Buck privates don't do that sort of thing to non-commissioned officers. I elected to take a more passive course. I would lie there until the corporal rolled over and then, seizing the opportunity, would quickly slip out of his grasp. But he was out cold. So I continued lying there, rigid as a board, listening to the clackety-clack of the train's wheels. Pretty soon I dozed off, but the corporal never awakened, never rolled over. I was the prisoner of compartment B, locked in the amorous embrace of a loved-starved corporal. If being able to sleep on troop trains was a prerequisite for service in the transportation corps, this corporal had stellar qualifications because when I awakened at daylight, the corporal still had me pinned squarely to the mat while continuing to sleep soundly.

The following evening, I asked Bruce if he'd like the lower berth. I explained that it wasn't fair for me to have the benefit of the lower every night. He consented, but the next morning as I sat across from him in the dining car, I saw a puzzled look on his face.

"Howja sleep last night?" I asked.

"Pretty good," he said, "not great."

"How come?"

"I dunno."

"Too crowded?" I asked.

He stared at me quizically.

"How come you asked me that?"

"Just wondered," I said in mock innocence.

"The hell you did."

"What?"

"The hell you did," he repeated.

"Do you think he was queer?"

"I hope not," he said. "He told me he was married."

"That doesn't mean anything," I said.

"Well, I don't give a damn if he is or isn't. You tricked me last night. Tonight it's your turn."

"Oh, Jesus."

"Don't worry," he said, "he's probably just homesick."

"Yeah, I'll keep that in mind."

Thinking about that time on the train, I recalled the beginning of Moby Dick. Ishmael recounts an incident that occurred in a rooming house in Nantucket while he was awaiting a berth on a whaling ship. The inn is overcrowded with seaman and Ishmael is forced to sleep in the same bed with the harpooner, Queequeg, a huge tattooed Indian who sleeps with his tomahawk. Ishmael awakens in the night, as terrified as I had been on the train, to find the ferocious looking Indian "embracing him in a loving and affectionate manner." As Ishmael reflects, "you'd almost think I had been his wife."

Bruce and I remained close friends throughout the war and afterwards. But he was not a regular reunion-goer, and after our St. Louis meeting in the early seventies, he stopped attending. From then on we went our separate ways. Bruce, only lately, has started to attend the reunions, bringing along his second wife, Colleen.

In the late sixties, Bruce and his first wife, Alma, came to Chicago to visit my wife and me. He had been a quiet, serious-minded fellow through the war, and had changed very little. Alma, however, seemed much more outgoing, and I remember being quite taken with her. She had written a novel, a very good one, entitled *A Gradual Joy*. It was published under the name of Alma Routsong, probably her maiden name.

They were divorced many years ago, and Bruce, who became a veterinarian, went on to teach Veterinary Medicine at the University of Illinois in Champaign. Alma became an editor in New York, and only recently passed away.

Late in the spring of 1943, the newly formed 124th AAA Gun Battalion (Mbl) at Camp Haan, California, received 616 enlisted men from Camp Callan, most from California, and a few, including me, from the midwest. A short time later another 161 enlisted men arrived from Camp Wallace, Texas, virtually all from Texas and Oklahoma. A cadre of 111 enlisted men and three medics were already present along with 29 officers. Lt. Colonel Carl M. Wood was the commanding officer, Major James R. Laney, Jr, the executive officer.

Camp Haan was everything Camp Callan wasn't — a barren and scrubby encampment where the unpleasant grind of preparing for war was all-consuming, and the likelihood of impending death or maiming frighteningly present night and day. But not for me, I would tell myself, not for a nice Jewish boy from a kosher home. Things like that don't happen to guys like me. Or do they? The thought was a disturbing one.

March Field, just across the road from Camp Haan, was an air force training base for B-24 Liberators. With their four engines roaring and their six turrets revealing 50-calibre machine guns and their bomb-bay doors open, ready to angle 1000-pound bombs toward their targets, these massive machines of destruction were constant reminders that we were involved in the serious business of killing.

We trained at Camp Haan for over six months, the battalion moving repeatedly from there to Camp Irwin, the latter a desert firing range north of Barstow, where we were trained in small arms fire and the operation of our basic weapon, the 90mm anti-air-craft/anti-tank gun. I vividly remember the hikes, 15 milers and 25 milers, none of which I completed. What the hell! Why finish the hikes? I was tired, and could always have the meat wagon pick me up. No wonder that I was always on Joe Snopek's shitlist or wilting under the angry glare of Captain Smith, the battery commander.

One afternoon during our 50th reunion in Riverside, I was hanging out in the lobby of the Hilton with some of the other men, waiting to join up with Bo Smith. Over the years, Bo and I have become good friends, and as we have often done at reunions were going out for a short run. Presently, he arrived. We were wearing our running gear. Evidently, he caught a glimpse of my 1986 Boston Marathon T-shirt.

"Can you imagine that Marks," he said to the men, "he's run

18 marathons and wasn't able to finish a single hike in the army."

Nothing that took place in the army is ever forgotten, my aborted hikes as well as my three-day pass for the Jewish holidays.

It was while I was at Camp Haan that I fell in love with two different women. I was already in love with Anita, in love with her letters and the memory of the times we spent together in L.A. My two new loves, however, were on the screen, Ella Raines and Deanna Durbin. My affection for them was the result of repeated exposure. To Miss Raines, a gaunt brunette, through many viewings of *Tall in the Saddle* in which she co-starred with John Wayne, and to Miss Durbin, fresh-faced and cherubic, through near-nightly viewings of *His Butler's Sister*. I figure that I saw each movie at least a dozen times. I remember going to the recreation hall after the movies and writing letters to them at Universal or Paramount studios, as the case may have been. "Dear Miss Durbin, I would begin, "I have never written a fan letter to anyone. You are absolutely the first, and I don't think I'll ever write to anyone else..." I remember being unhappy with that opening, and I would tear up the letter and start again. "Dear Miss Durbin, I am not accustomed to writing fan letters to people in the motion picture business but quite by accident I caught your film..." And that too was torn up. In fact, I never mailed any letters to either of the two movie stars. All of them wound up in the waste basket, and none got any farther than the first or second sentence because I couldn't come up with an opening that didn't sound like the words of a lovesick jerk.

I shared a pup tent with Eddie Maxwell during our desert training at Camp Irwin. We're good friends now, but weren't back then. Our teaming up was purely a result of alphabetical order. We slept side by side, with only the center pole of the tent separating our sleeping bags. He was a kid from the backwoods of Louisiana who had never seen a Jew before, let alone shared a tent with one. We had in common only a mistrust of each other and a fear of scorpions and tarantulas. At night, we searched our sleeping bags with painstaking thoroughness, and once satisfied that the bags were free of the poisonous varmints, we searched them again, just to make sure. Neither of us had ever discovered these lethal visitors in our sacks, but many was the morning that we awakened, freezing in the cold desert air, to find our boots gone, dragged away in the middle of the night by pack rats, and left out in the desert.

Our training at Camp Irwin was beginning to show results. The men on the gun crews had speeded up their loading and firing times, while as for myself, A Battery's so-called scouting and patrolling expert, I was able to go off into the desert with some K-rations, a compass and a canteen of water and eventually find my way back to camp. I fancied myself a real killer, itching to attach a bayonet to my M-1 rifle and go hunting for Krauts. On reflection, it was the ultimate in self-delusion for at that time my physical courage had never been tested.

General George Patton was at the time in command of ground combat forces in the U.S., and we were among his charges. General Leslie McNair was either about to invade North Africa or had already done so. In any case, rumors were floating around Camp Irwin that we were heading for Oran. I would be in good company with either Patton or McNair.

Meanwhile, we continued to shuttle between Camp Haan and Camp Irwin. The most painful of these journeys was from Haan to Irwin. Each mile brought me deeper into the desert, farther away from Anita and deeper into isolation and loneliness. We rumbled along in our 2 1/2-ton trucks through the small desert community of Victorville, and from there into Barstow, an equally small desert outpost. But it was the last 35 miles of the trip, on the rough road north through the desert from Barstow to Camp Irwin, that was particularly agonizing. I had been within striking distance of Hollywood and Anita, but now I was leaving all that behind, replacing it with my cajun tent-mate, Eddie Maxwell. Anita! Anita! An echo that was fading away. I wrote to her almost every night. The one time I was given a weekend pass I hitchhiked back to Riverside to catch the Pacific Electric train to L.A. It took hours, a journey to test the love of any man. For that occasion I would scrub my khakis with G.I. soap and, before rinsing them, spread them to dry in the desert sun. It made them fade evenly and take on a salty appearance so that I looked like an old trooper who had served at Pearl. It was a trick I had picked up from the regular army guys who had been stationed at Schofield Barracks.

Anita and I would walk together down Hollywood Boulevard or stand in front of the Brown Derby on Vine, watching for movie stars. But most of the time I just waited for her to finish her stint at the Hollywood Canteen where she was a hostess on weekends. "Won't you tell me when," Nan Wynn would sing on the jukeboxes, "we will meet again, Sunday, Monday or always?" The song was played so often it became part of Anita. She was tall, older than I, and far wiser. She had sharp features and soft blond hair, and was very kind to me. Later, she wrote to me regularly in England, France and Germany, and I wept at night at the thought of her.

We left California in early February, 1944, our training almost over. I was nearly in tears. There would be no more passes to Los Angeles. Goodbye, Main Street. Goodbye to that wonderful old train, the Pacific Electric, that carried me back and forth to downtown L.A. So long Hollywood, the center of the universe, glamorous, romantic Hollywood. So long Sheldon Leonard, you in your white apron washing dishes and serving the soldiers at the Hollywood Canteen, and goodbye especially to Anita. I was never to see her again.

For the next five weeks we were shuttled from one army camp to another on the east coast. I flunked hikes, as usual, pulled KP, as usual, incurred the disdain of Joe Snopek and Bo Smith, as usual. I was a fuckup par excellence, cocky and incorrigible, and it still surprises me that I wasn't transferred to some fuckup outfit. What patience and tolerance the captain and the sergeant showed. Maybe, even at that time, there was some mysterious force at work pronouncing me a lifelong member of the brotherhood of the 124th, never to be separated from the group until death intervened.

On a bright summer morning, about a month after D-Day, the battalion arrived at the Port of Debarkation in Liverpool. When we docked, there were 686 enlisted men and 29 officers in the battalion. Liverpool presented a majestic spectacle with imposing buildings all along the waterfront. It was a sunny day, ships and boats of all sizes and types crowded the harbor, and the homes and buildings in the background made the entire setting seem near magical. Perhaps, on reflection, the harbor was not really as spectacular as it seemed at the time. I would have been happy to see land of any kind after six seasick days at sea. I had slept on a hammock of sorts directly against the ship's hull. It was not a good location. There was plenty of enemy action in the North Atlantic, and had we been hit by a torpedo, it would have been curtains for all of us.

About two weeks later, on July 22, 1944, forty-six days after the invasion at Omaha Beach, the battalion took up its position in Kent, on the southeast coast of Britain. There was violent ground combat raging along the hedgerows of Normandy, just across the channel. Meantime, at our position, which was aptly described by the British as "Hellfire-Corner," an area along the west side of the channel extending from Dover on the north to Lands End on the south, hell was raging in the sky. Communities in between — Folkestone, Hythe, New Romney, Romney Marsh and Lidd — were getting a steady pasting, and, as if to mitigate the horror of it all, we were being treated nightly to a breathtaking light show in which 50-calibre tracers criss-crossed the heavens, bisecting in weird linear patterns the exploding bursts of the ack-ack shells. The second Battle of Britain was in progress. London and the southeast corner of Britain were being pounded by an onslaught of V-1 rockets, known variously as doodlebugs, divers, and robots. The V-1's droned across the sky, at fixed altitudes, bound for London. But often the droning sound stopped just over us, directly over my head, so it seemed. The drone was suddenly replaced by the most eerie silence I can recall. It was as if the world had abruptly gone silent, the gulls in the channel had stopped shrieking, and all other life screeched to a halt. Somewhere in the clouds a V-1 rocket was hurtling to earth, condemning us to death if it fell anywhere near us. But then suddenly the silence would end, and a rocket would fall to earth, close enough for us to hear the explosion but far enough away to give us a reprieve. "Thanks, Lord, I would swear, I'll make it up to you."

The 124th and five other American ack-ack battalions were attached to the 55th British Brigade under Brigadier General Pyle. We were dispersed to various locations along the coast, each gun battery located a few miles from the other. I was working on the plotting board in the computer, tracking the locations of the V-1's on their westward course toward London.

Around this time, I made two trips to London on pass. I felt lonely and overwhelmed by the city, and so I did what most American soldiers did — congregated around Rainbow Corner, a premier USO club in Picadilly. There were paratroopers and fly boys, infantrymen, sailors, WAC's, WREN's and army nurses — nearly every branch of service was represented. The men looked tough, battle-scarred or battle-worthy, and they were out for a roaring good time. There I was among them, a scrawny pfc whose o.d. uniform was especially drab, devoid of any decorations at all except for my lonely marksman's medal. I looked like a displaced person and felt like one. I played ping-pong much of the time, rarely winning a match. Although I'm considered a good player, I found it hard to concentrate in the face of all the activity taking place on the street. There were plenty of girls to be picked up in Picadilly, slatternly types with bad teeth, but girls nonetheless — another contest to engage in besides ping-pong — and I would have sold my soul just to buy one of them coffee — but I never emerged a winner in any of those contests either.

Defeated by nightfall, I would stop by the men's room in the Strand Palace Hotel and watch some of the high-rollers shooting crap before catching the train back to Kent, my hand all the while, tightly clutching the five-pound note I wouldn't have parted with, no matter what the odds.

London, at this time, was involved in another kind of strife besides bombings. It took place between black and white servicemen. The army was carefully segregated, the blacks, for the most part, performing behind-the-lines service work — construction, enginneering, and so on, while caucasians and other non-black troops, largely comprised our fighting forces. The war had brought each group, black and white, out of their cultural cocoons, the innate prejudices of the southern white now colliding suddenly with the new found "freedom" of the black. Beatings and homicides were not uncommon. While the prostitutes flouncing down Shaftesbury avenue did not set out deliberately to aggravate the problem, they were indirectly responsible for it.

Anita continued to write, but I found someone closer to focus on. Her name was Diane. She was in the Women's Land Army, a non-military group of farm workers who lived in the surrounding area. We first met late one afternoon in a tea shop in Hythe. She was bicycling home, back to Romney Marsh, having stopped for tea. The WLA girls were unsung heroines. They replaced the men who were in the army. They tended sheep and did stenuous farm work, young girls doing men's work, and doing it well. They arrived at their assigned farms before sun up and didn't finish until late afternoon when they would bicycle back home.

My friendship with Diane was confined to early evening hours, after she finished her work. We walked along the cobblestone streets of Hythe, holding hands and making promises to each other, often stopping for tea at the shop where we first met. After dark, we made love in the surrounding fields. The canopy over our grass-covered bed was a sky filled with screaming tracer bullets. We didn't mind. It was a protest of sorts, on the need to make love, not war.

She was short and heavy-set and her brown woolen uniform was unbecoming. But she had a pretty face and a sweet smile. Our unit left for Southhampton in September on our way to Normandy. "Take good care of yourself," she said as I kissed her goodbye." We were both 19.

I returned to Dover late in 1994 for the 50th anniversaary of the Battle of Britain. It was a British celebration for the troops who fought at "Hellfire Corner." Six American ack-ack battalions were guests, ours among them. The turnout of Americans, however, was dismal. Bo Smith and I were the only men from A Battery. Too many of the men had passed away or were too ill or too broke to travel.

There was a banquet at the Dover Town Hall nearly every evening of our six day stay. Most of the British veterans who attended had served with the Royal Artillery, the most favored and most elite of the British troops. The climax of every evening was dancing. The orchestra played Glenn Miller numbers from the war. As expected, a recording of Vera Lynn's rendition of *White Cliffs of Dover* filled the hall each time the orchestra went on break. The old British soldiers wearing blue blazers and regimental striped ties sagged under the weight of the medals adorning their jackets. There were plenty of gray haired old ladies around, many of them widows or spinsters. They had served with the ATS or the Women's Land Army. They danced with some of the unattached veterans. Often they danced with one another. I danced with a number of them. The music was slow and very sad and as we danced it was as if it were 1944 again when ack-ack shells jolted a war-weary sky, when no one counted too much on seeing tomorrow arrive. Diane could have been in that room. I asked if anyone knew her. I kept asking until I began to feel foolish. In a way I was glad I didn't find her.

In the dank, labyrinthine corridors below Dover Castle, a medieval fortress near the sea, were the remnants of the nerve center of the British command. I had visited it while I was at Dover. All of the equipment was still in place, covered with dust and cobwebs. Here in that damp place was where the British controlled the Battle of Britain. So this is where they all came from, those messages and test transmissions that came over the 543 radio I had manned while seated at night on the plotting board. It was from here, this dark, hell-hole that they came, and not, as I had then thought, from some beautifully upholstered war room somewhere.

As I stood there looking at the antiquated equipment, the voices I once heard returned, seemingly filling the room, as clear and clipped as fifty years before.

Hello, Romo, this is Buttercup.
Hello, Romo, this is Buttercup.

There was never a reply, just the same refrain over and over, a monotonous but nevertheless welcome companion through the long nights of bombing. And then another voice, plaintive and hushed:

> The following is a test transmission. June
> deposited her money at the ticket office
> and walked into the theater. It was extremely
> dark inside. She groped her way down the aisle
> until she found a seat. Suddenly she felt
> someone's presence beside her. She looked up.
> "Conroy," she breathed.

And there were the other voices that came from across the channel — those of Lord Haw Haw and Axis Sally, and the one still lodged in my memory, never to be forgotten:

> Achtung, Luftwaffe, Achtung Luftwaffe
> Kein flugzeuge uber der Ruhr Gewiet
> Kein flugzeuge uber der Ruhr Gewiet

Today there is a plaque on a wall in the castle's dungeon. It reads:

> To Commemorate
> The 120th, 124th, 125th, 126th, 127th, 134th
> AAA Gun Battalions, US Army
> which were controlled from
> this Castle Headquarters during
> OPERATION CROSSBOW
> in combat against
> the V1 Flying Bombs
> and were credited with a total of
> 854 kills
> during the summer of 1944

The Battle of Britain left London in shambles. Large parts of the southeast coast of Britain were demolished. In the few months that we were operational, we engaged 1100 targets, enemy aircraft and

V-1's alike, and in the process fired off 30,000 rounds of 90mm ammunition and a like amount of .50 caliber machine gun ammo. Innocent lives were lost, homes were destroyed, and the topography desecrated. Amidst such horror only the unconquerable spirit of the British people remained miraculously in tact.

FOUR

Back in Scottsdale, Bowen Smith, looking elegant and trim, arrived for the reunion the day after my arrival, wearing khaki slacks, a long-sleeved rayon sports shirt, and loafers. A long-time Californian, he dressed in tasteful Ivy League West clothing, and for all his years still looked like a young man. I never realized it until recently, but while watching Senior Golf on TV I was struck by how much my old battery commander resembled the fiftysomething golfer, Hale Irwin. We chatted briefly and I made a date to have breakfast with him the following morning.

I drove him to Katz's delicatessen on Central avenue in Phoenix. It was a mischievous choice, Katz's being a downscale, poorly appointed deli whose one and only virtue was good food. It had been around Phoenix for years and I had made it a point to have either breakfast or lunch there whenever I was in town. It reminded me of the Phoenix I had known many years before.

Bo was a true WASP and regular army man, a classic of the species. He was also a good guy. I didn't think so in the beginning but once he was back in civilian clothes he became the best friend I could ask for. He did not especially relish unusual food, especially the kind of kosher-style food they served at Katz's, but he finally settled for bacon and eggs. He had only recently lost his younger brother, a college professor, and, in spite of his usual stoicism, I could tell he was having a hard time dealing it. He had written me late that summer about his brother and sent me a copy of the eulogy his brother's wife had delivered. Several years earlier, Bo's younger son, Lance, had been killed in an auto accident. His remaining child, Noel, a dentist, had just gone through a painful divorce. Bo and his wife, Diana, had had some tough breaks, but he never told me how deeply he felt about his troubles, merely stated the facts as though he were a supply sergeant ticking off items on an equipment list.

When I first met him, Bo was the battery commander of A Battery. He was then about 23, perhaps five years older than I, a tall handsome young captain with a gaunt face and slightly over-large ears. What struck me about him at the time was how solemn he was. He never cracked a smile, never uttered a lighthearted word. He seldom spoke at any length to the troops, merely stated his case, issued orders, but left it to Joe Snopek to fill in the details and carry them out. His body, however, did most of the talking. He strode about arrogantly, in a somewhat ungainly lope, his arms dangling loosely. From his manner you'd think he was a West Pointer. Everything by the book; every movement by the numbers, often to the point of foolishness. Take the simple matter of syn-chronizing watches. Bo would fling out his arm like a boxer throw-ing a left jab. (one-two). Once his arm was fully extended, he would then bend it at the elbow at a perfect 45-degree angle (three-four) and abruptly draw it back toward his body (five-six) where he would read his wrist watch. Even today, when I want to find out the time, I find myself emulating Bo's motion. The four other battery commanders were first lieutenants, and the way I had things figured — only by being a West Pointer could Bo have come by his higher rank. I was dead wrong. As I later found out he had received his OCS commission at Camp Davis, North Carolina, at the Coast Artillery school. As for his manner, I sup-pose it was just a case of his trying to prove, in his own youthful way, that he was worthy of his captaincy.

Bo never acknowledged my presence. He had a way of look-ing at me by looking through me, as though eye contact with me, a lowly enlisted man, might somehow establish familiarity. He knew my name but that's as far as it went. Nevertheless, I had a grudging admiration for him, and for that reason I studied him carefully. I noticed that he was every bit as reserved with the other officers as he was with me and the other enlisted men, and I imagined that even when he was alone with fellow officers he maintained the same reserve. I also learned that he corresponded throughout the war with a woman named Diana whom I later came to know through our reunions. They were married after the war, at the Mission Inn in Riverside. It was proof, after all, that he was human. Still, in our three years together during the war, we hardly exchanged a word.

At our reunions, the early ones at least, I kept my distance from him. I was intimidated by officers, and especially by him. We talked some but he still had that way of looking through me when he spoke. At one of our reunions in St. Louis, in 1968, he finally acknowledged that he knew me, as a person. We were having drinks in the hospitality suite at our hotel. The room was crowded, filled with cigarette smoke. Suddenly I felt a poke on my backside — not a goose, just a good-natured thump. I abruptly swung around. Bo was behind me, laughing. So were some of the men. Bo, as a gag, had attached a toilet plunger to the end of a broomstick and then attached the A battery guidon to the plunger. I didn't get the joke, but I joined in the laughter anyway. I seemed to have had no choice, the gag being the brainstorm of my former commanding officer. As Bo later explained, many years earlier when we were training at Camp Haan I had been carrying the battery guidon on a parade ground march. Bo, wearing his full regalia, was leading the battery, when accidentally I let the pole holding the guidon drop down to a point nearly parallel with the ground, in the process jabbing Bo in the rear. He had never forgotten the incident, and in his own way, I think, was reaching out to me in a gesture of friendship and recognition, the first such gesture in the 25 years I had known him.

In Europe during the war, Bo was an unsmiling no-nonsense taskmaster. I'll grant that his responsibilities were enormous. There was the matter of protecting our supply lines from German airstrikes, for in war's football field we would be considered the safety backs. Out ahead of us, and closer to the enemy, were mortars, light artillery, tanks and infantry, any of which could be, and often were, leap-frogged by bomb-laden German aircraft. If there was one thing Bo wouldn't tolerate it was any kind of a tactical fuckup, major or minor, and as far as I knew none had ever occurred. In fact, of the six ack-ack battalions assigned to bring down V-I bombs during the Battle of Britain, the 124th, and more specifically, A Battery, with Bo in charge, had more kills than any of the other 23 batteries involved.

I frequently pulled duty in the computer, a mobile power source, hooked up to our radar. The computer itself was a trailer. It held two or three men and a plotting board, the latter linked manually to data fed by the radar. It was my job to man the plotting board, spotting the locations of enemy aircraft. Once the range and altitude of the aircraft had been determined, the officer on duty could, at the appropriate time, give the command to fire. I must say that when Bo was on duty, the computer became a silent tomb, an instrument of cold-blooded efficiency. He rarely spoke to me except to give an order or to ask an official question. Perhaps that was as it should be. But when I think about the friends we've become in our later years, Bo's behavior then was in striking contrast to the way he behaves toward me today. It continues to astound me that this man has become such a close friend. I find it

Bo never acknowledged my presence. He had a way of looking at me by looking through me, as though eye contact with me, a lowly enlisted man, might somehow establish familiarity. He knew my name but that's about as far as it went.

even more difficult to understand when I think about the time in Holland when, frustrated by my indolence, Bo picked up a gas mask and threw it in my face.

At our reunions over the years, Bo, Diana and I became a team. We shared the same table at our Saturday night banquets, and many years ago when we had live or canned music at the banquets, Diana and I would dance together. Then as now she is a beautiful woman, blond, lithe and of a romantic nature, revealed in part by her love of writing. I always wondered how she was able to hit it off with Bo, a man seemingly so unlike her. My wife would sometimes attend with me, and on those occasions the four of us became a congenial foursome.

When the battalion returned to Riverside in 1993 for our 50th reunion, neither my wife nor Diana attended. I recall having checked into the Riverside Hilton and being handed a message by the desk clerk. It was from Bo. Would I consider sharing a room with him? At first my reaction was to say no. I was pleased that he made the offer, but I didn't want any of my buddies to find out that I, a pfc draftee, was bunking with a colonel. I was sure they would regard me as a traitor even though the time has long passed when I would have been called brown-nose or suck-ass. Nevertheless, I didn't want my fellow enlisted men to feel that I

I learned that he corresponded throughout the war with a woman named Diana whom I later came to know during our reunions. They were married after the war at the Mission Inn in Riverside, California. It was proof after all that he was human.

was aspiring to a higher social standing in the army. I was one of them, they were my brothers, the men I felt most comfortable with. For them to find out that I was bunking with the colonel would have been a terrible affront to them and an embarassment to me.

But I quickly remembered that there was no longer such a thing as rank in our invisible army, this gathering of old men. There are no gold or silver bars, no gold leafs, no stripes. We are mere remnants of the past, all equal, with nothing more than shared memories to bring us together. Bo is part of that memory, and if I wanted to bunk with him, who cares? But on the other hand whom am I kidding? What about that little voice inside my head that tells me that enlisted men do not consort with officers. Not back then, and not now. No exceptions to the rule. I am, alas, a hapless victim of the army caste system. It had grabbed hold of me at 18 and it still won't let go.

But there I was. For the next two nights Bo and I holed up in a suite at the Riverside Hilton, he in the bedroom, I on a fold-away couch in the living room. The next morning, shortly after I got up, Bo came into the living room and began making my bed. Embarrassed, I immediately pitched in to help, but he waved me off. It wasn't that he was playing supplicant — just being a true army man, trying to get the room in shape, and it didn't make any difference if I was a pfc or a general. But all I could think of at the time was Irving Berlin's World War 1 song, "I've Got My Captain Working For Me Now."

After the 124th was disbanded in 1945, Bo, Joe Snopek, and a few other officers and non-coms were reassigned as cadre to the 72nd Infantry, and that's where the trail ended for my two oppressors. Most of us, as I had mentioned, were shipped home a few months later, but Bo and my old topkick were out of my life for the next quarter of a century. I next saw Joe in 1968, and Bo at the same time. Joe was subsequently discharged, but Bo became the quintessential army regular, serving in the South Pacific, in Korea, in Viet Nam, at the Pentagon and at the Command and General Staff College, Diane the dutiful army wife always at his side. Bo eventually became a bird colonel, and his final army gig was as Professor of Military Science at Claremont College in Pomona, his duty there coming during the student riots of the 1960's, a most unpleasant time for anyone to be in charge of an ROTC program.

When it was announced that the 124th was invited to the celebration of the second Battle of Britain in 1994, I was one of the first to sign up, but only after I was prevailed upon by Bo to come along. Bo, I would wager, was the first to send in his name. There were six American ack-ack battalions represented but only an aggregate of 25 men showed up. According to the plan, we were to meet at a hotel in London near Hyde Park, and from there would be transported by lorry to Dover, the site of the celebration. When we arrived at our hotel in Dover, I spotted Bo, who had arrived a day earlier, nervously pacing the parking lot looking for me. When I alighted from the bus, Bo was smiling, evidently pleased that I had arrived without fucking up. I had brought along one large suitcase. My room was on the fourth floor, but the hotel lift was out of order, and my only recourse, barring sitting around in the lobby until the lift was fixed, was to take the stairs. I grabbed my suitcase and was about to start the climb, when Bo came up alongside me, took the suitcase and seemingly without effort walked up the four flights, my luggage in hand. As I walked along beside him, the words to the old Irving Berlin classic once again started running through my mind.

The parade through the streets of Dover was the high point of the Dover celebration. We American ack-ack soldiers joined forces with British artillery units, the ATS women and the WLA workers. There were several British regimental bands on hand and virtually the entire population of Dover lined the streets cheering us on. The Lord Mayor of Dover, local dignitaries, British army generals and Lady Mountbatten, the widow of Lord Louis Mountbatten, were positioned in the reviewing stand. It was a glorious day. The sun was shining. Bo Smith, resplendent in his full dress blues, his military ribbons covering his chest like corn rows, was enjoying his finest hour. Just such a moment as this is what he lived for, what we all lived for. I was wearing my red artillery cap and my own rather meager military ribbons. It was a day to dream about, to remember forever. We Americans marched in three files, following an air force contingent carrying the American flag. As we came into view, the applause burst out like thunder along the channel sea wall. We had some difficulty keeping in step. I don't think any of us had marched in over fifty years. With all the skipping and changing of stride in order to get in step, we looked like two-dozen participants in a mass hop-scotch tournament. It was a sorry performance, and it appeared as though we would never establish a cadence. But then suddenly a near miracle occurred. The reviewing stand came into view, the music became louder, the applause even more deafening, and twenty-five old men suddenly fell into step, threw back their shoulders and strutted proudly past the reviewing stand, the inside file looking smartly to its right as they passed — at Lady Mountbatten, Vice Lord Lieutenant of Kent; at Admiral of the Fleet Sir William Staveley; at General Sir Martin Farndale, Master Gunner St. James Park; and at Air Commodore C.R. Spink.

After the parade, there was a luncheon gathering at a picnic ground on the outskirts of Dover. There were British soldiers from World War II, together with troops presently stationed at the Dover garrison. The WRENS, the ATS and WLA ladies were there, their faces lined with age. There were a few high ranking American military attaches who had come down from London. The British generals were there, and so was Lady Mountbatten. The brigadier in charge of the Dover garrison, a young elegant military man with an angry red birthmark on the nape of his neck was the man supervising the proceedings. A day earlier he had pinned a Battle of Britain commendation medal on each of us Americans, and we had also received a lapel pin reading "White Cliff Veterans of Hell-Fire Corner," named aptly for the violent air-artillery action over the English Channel in the summer of 1944. Along the line I became an honorary member of the British Legion, which carries about as much distinction as my American Legion pin. A lot of trinkets for being in Dover at the right time but even so you might be surprised to know the value they take on, even for one as cynical as I, when you grow old and find that most of your thoughts revolve around having served in the "good war."

A week earlier, when I had arrived at Heathrow on my way to Dover, I took the underground to a stop closest to the hotel where I was to join up with the other Americans. From there I took a taxi to the hotel. The driver was an amiable fellow, perhaps in his early fifties. He asked what brought me to London, and I explained that I was here for the 50th anniversary of the Battle of Britain. Seemingly overjoyed that he had such a celebrated fare, he abruptly pulled his taxi over to the curb, then turned, beaming, oblivious to the traffic, and shook my hand in appreciation, thanking me for what I had done for his country. Fifty years after the war had ended, this wonderful man was expressing his appreciation. It touched me more deeply than than any of the tokens that I was later to receive from the British government, more deeply in fact than any expression of thanks from our own government, more than any emoluments such as veterans' bonuses or a paid-for education on the G.I. Bill. When we arrived at the hotel, he got out of the taxi, shook my hand again, and pressed a commemorative Battle of Britain coin into my palm.

The story does not end there. I registered with one of the women in the hotel lobby, and then took a seat and awaited the arrival of the lorries to drive us to Dover. Well over an hour had gone by, and still no lorries. Then suddenly I looked up. There was my taxi driver, standing there sheepishly, having been escorted to my chair by the woman who signed me in. Almost apologetically, he handed me my passport. I had left it on the back seat of his cab, and when one of his passengers had discovered it, he had driven back to the hotel, hoping that he'd still find me there. Had he not found the passport, there would have been, for one small thing, no trip across the channel to Normandy where we were to receive a decoration from the French government. No matter that the ceremony was subsequently cancelled.

Back at the picnic grounds, I had lost sight of Bo the moment the lorries dropped us off. I strolled around aimlessly, chatting with some of our ack-ack troops, had a paper plate of food, then ambled casually over to a large tent where Lady Mountbatten and the various brass were having lunch. In their midst was Bo in his full dress army blues, along with his blue garrison cap. He was talking with Lady Mountbatten. I overheard snippets of his conversation, which dealt with his wife's British relatives. After awhile he moved on, and then called me over to meet the Dover brigadier and an American miliary attache. I could tell that Bo wasn't finished mingling with the brass, many of them a generation younger than he. So I moved on, and then later caught a ride back to the hotel. Later that afternoon, he called me to fill me in on his converation with Lady Mountbatten, his voice filled with pride.

Everyone wants to matter. It's part of the human condition. Bo, I, and the men of the 124th are no different. We feel the need ever more poignantly each year. You see it in many of us at every Memorial Day and Flag Day parade and in every 4th of July celebration. You don't have to ask us twice to put on our overseas caps and medals and strut our stuff. Having fought in the war, and having actually been in the thick of it all, was our greatest accomplishment. But that was a long time ago. We're old now. We don't work. Most of the men are ill. We're getting poorer. Nobody listens to what we have to say; nobody pays attention. Where do you go anymore to earn a merit badge, to have something to pin on your chest, something to tell the world that you do matter. So once a year we have a reunion, or else we return to the scene of our finest hour, as Bo and I did in Dover, and for a few short days we're soldiers again, and we're important, and we do matter.

One day during the early days of Desert Shield, just after we began sending troops to Saudi Arabia, the doorman at the apartment building where I live, stopped me as I was leaving the building. An immigrant from Hungary, about my age, he had fought on the Russian front during World War II. I was never sure on which side, and never pressed the matter.

"Mister," he said, "you and me, ve go down to the army place. Ve enlist."

We had talked before about the war, and he knew that I was in Europe in 1944 and 1945.

"Are you kidding?" I said.

"No, no," he said, "you and me, ve show those kids. Tibor and the mister, ve still got what it takes." He nudged me in the ribs, then hunched up his shoulders and curled his forearms into a strong-like-bull pose.

"Who'd want us, Tibor," I said, "wars are for young guys, not old bucks like us."

"You think it over, mister, you and me, ve go together."

In a crazy way, his idea had appeal. I had nothing important to occupy my time, and I had been longing to get into action ever since I began easing into retirement. But to do what? I was a has-been, too old to fight, another invisible man with too much time on his hands, a piece of walking history. It wasn't so long ago that I was carrying an overstuffed briefcase into mahogany board rooms, dashing through airports, spouting memos into a portable dictating machine, but those days are behind me.

I remember the movie, *The Roaring Twenties*. Jimmy Cagney, an ex-mobster, lies dead on the steps of a church, gunned down moments before by hired killers. His old flame, Gladys George, cradles him in her arms. A cop shows up. "Who is this guy," he asks. "This is Eddie Bartlett," she says, her voice swelling with pride. "Yeah," says the cop, "what was his business?" Fighting back her tears, she says, "he used to be a big-shot."

And so it is with me.

During the next few weeks I got caught up in the excitement of Desert Shield. It was just like the old days. Once again we were fighting a "good war." There were flags and ribbons and tearful goodbyes. Watching our troops on television brought memories of 1943 into focus. I could still feel the sand of Camp Irwin in my eyes and feel the weight of my helmet under the hot desert sun. The memory made me feel better about myself. I too had once stood tall and laughed in the face of danger, just as the troops had that I saw on TV.

In a sense, I found myself trying to relive the past. I began carrying a wallet size photostat of my army discharge. On the reverse side was my military record — my military specialty, the campaigns I participated in, the citations I received. It was if having my discharge with me would give my diminished self-esteem a needed boost.

One morning, a man I often have breakfast with in a restaurant downtown, steered our conversation about Desert Shield around to his own experiences in World War II. A former State Senator, he told me he had received a battlefield commission in the infantry. He wasn't talking only to me but to all who were within hearing range. He was well up in his seventies, a short heavy set man, Bernard Neistein by name, who perpetually chomped on an unlighted cigar. The next morning he returned to the restaurant, this time passing around photographs of himself in uniform.

What was he doing? The same thing I would be doing if I had removed my wallet and passed around my own military history — two old guys telling the world they used to be big shots. It was what my good friend Bo Smith was doing that week in Dover, wearing that outlandish out-of-phase uniform and mingling with the young brass. The reliving of old memories is not just for enlisted men like me, or for junior grade officers like my friend in the restaurant, but for the higher ranking officers like Colonel Bowen Noel Smith (ret.) a good guy who was once in line to become Brigadier General.

I often think of those moments when my emotions ran so high that I felt I would explode with pride, when the flesh tingled and the tears ran down my face. It would happen each time I finished a marathon, the cheering of the crowd ringing in my ears. The 1993 New York City Marathon which I had last run at age 69 was right up toward the top of my list of "highs." During the last few miles of the race many of the thousands of people lining the course in Central Park were cheering me on. "Come on, Pop," they yelled, as I struggled for breath. "Let's go Gramps," they screamed. And the people reached out to touch my hand and the young girls threw kisses at me, and miraculously the numbness left my legs and my breath came easier. Now there was an explosion of cheers from the crowd as I crossed the finish line, and I suddenly felt fresh and strong, yet unable to control the sobbing and trembling that wracked my body.

The following year in Dover was another such moment as we marched along the Dover seawall, passing in review before Britain's highest military brass, hearing the thunderous applause of the normally reserved English. And once again I felt wobbly from the spontaneous outburst of cheering, and I threw back my shoulders and felt the spring return to my tired old legs.

"In my end is my beginning," wrote T.S. Eliot. And so it was that in the late 1920's and early 1930's, when I was a young boy in Iowa, my mother would take me downtown to watch the parades on Decoration Day and Armistice Day. We would stand on the sidewalk, as close to the curb as we could get, my head no higher than my mother's waist. It was a stirring sight — the drum and bugle corps, the high school marching bands, the flags and banners and the high-stepping drum majors and majorettes. Then the men came, some in uniform but most wearing street clothes, their caps tilted at an angle, proudly wearing their medals. I stood there in wonder as they filed past. They stared straight ahead, heads held high, shoulders back, looking as though they were once again marching off to war. Some of the men were the age of my father, some the age of my great Uncle Abe. A few of the men were very old, veterans of the Civil War. I remember how those very old men looked, their eyes a pale, watery blue, their cheeks sunken, their mouths pinched. In spite of their pain and unsteadiness, they marched with determination and precision, acting as if they were young men performing close order drill.

Thinking back on the scene, I am sure that those old men who then walked strong and proud down Locust street in Des Moines had only the day before hobbled listlessly around their homes, cranky and ill. But those old soldiers, as I can now well attest, suddenly become resuscitated, their lives redefined, when they pick up the sound of drumbeats and see the color guard come into view and hear the band begin to play.

FIVE

There are gaps in my memory when I try to remember where I was at particular times and places in France, Holland and Germany. For this reason I have relied on a terse chronicle compiled by the late Clarence White, one of our A Battery lieutenants. It is our battalion Baedecker, giving dates and places, but little more than that. The real war, the one that happened somewhere between time and place, was so unrelentingly tedious for my fellow artilleryman and me that it would have been impossible to record. Each person's war is a highly personal affair, as different for me as it was for other soldiers. The incidents that I can't remember might very well be remembered by someone else. Those that I can remember could well be a blur to another man. What remains for me is a collection of out-of-the ordinary occurrences, memorable and meaningful to me alone because they hit me hard enough to remain vivid throughout the years. But like a photo album that holds undated snapshots, the memories lack sequence or connection. The ordinary things, those grimly repetitive details of living in danger and hardship can't, or won't, be recalled.

Combat for us during the fall and winter of 1944 and through the winter of 1945, was a continuous blur of bone-numbing cold, mud-soaked boots, frozen toes, and grime-covered longjohns. The days were bleak, the nights an endless blank. The uniform of the day was the uniform of every day — boots, long woolen overcoats covering field jackets, and o.d. pants and shirts. Our heads were covered with o.d. knit caps, helmet liners, and steel helmets. The helmets, in addition to their primary purpose, were used to urinate in, bathe in, and eat out of. Today when I walk into the restroom of a restaurant and see a sign that says "Employees Must Wash Hands Before Returning To Work," I can't help but smile at the thought of the cooks in our makeshift field kitchens. We had showers twice in six months' time, once when a portable shower unit, an all-black detachment commanded by a white officer, arrived at our position somewhere in Germany, and earlier when we were hauled off to Brussels to be de-loused and given a hot shower and a fresh uniform.

Along with that shower, there was an unforgettable 12-hours in Brussels, a welcome reprieve from over three months' combat in Holland. Several 2 1/2-ton trucks had carried us off the line and into Brussels, finally dropping us off in front of a *gymnasium* where we were to be purged of three-months' accumulation of filth. Be mindful that it was the winter of 1945 and frightfully cold. No one had bathed during that bitter winter; nor had our long underwear been changed — actually a special benefit — because the accumulated grime on the cloth acted as additional insulation against the cold.

Our trucks were parked less than a block from the *gymnasium*. We had the whole day and much of the evening on our own, but if we hadn't returned to the trucks by 10 that evening for the ride back to Holland we would be considered AWOL.

Along with two companions, I headed straight for the shower. But our progress was interrupted when we spotted a bar a few doors away. Very dirty but also very thirsty, we decided on the drink first. We walked into the bar and found a table. Three bar girls swooped down on us immediately. The one who selected me was not pretty. She had dark hair and small pointed breasts, and what she lacked in looks she made up for in brazenness. I finished my cognac, and she led me up a flight of stairs to a comfortable looking room and immediately reached into my trousers. Handicapped by the language barrier, I tried to let her know that it had been many weeks since I had bathed. "Please, please," I pleaded. "I'll be back, later, later!" But she just nodded her head, uncomprehendingly. My high school French had failed me miserably, and I suddenly understood why French was a required language. While I continued to protest, she calmly went about her work. Once on her bed, all fight went out of me. Finally, after I put on my trousers, I paid her what she asked, said *"mercii, madmoiselle,"* and walked down the stairway and out the door. Moments later, I turned in my uniform to a gymnasium attendant, and walked into stall where I was de-loused with DDT. Soon, I was relaxing under the hot shower I'd been dreaming about, the hot water pouring over me, the cognac warming my insides. Finally, cleansed and purified, all thoughts of the war and the obliging barmaid washed down the drain, I reluctantly turned off the shower.

That evening, I found myself at Club Corso, a boisterous Brussels nightclub where I was taken by a young woman whom I had met somewhere on the street. She was pretty and plump and had straight black hair, and was friendly to the Americans — but not that friendly. During the evening, a civilian — a Belgian, I'm quite sure — approached our table. He stood staring at me, and then suddenly shouted, *"Landsman,"* a German-Yiddish word for "countryman." We shook hands, and he moved off into the crowd. Who he was, where he came from, and how he picked me out as a Jew, puzzled me then and continues to puzzle me today.

So when you ask me about those out-of-ordinary events that I still think about, ask me about that. But ask me, if you want to, about the shooting side of the war and I won't be able to supply you with many details. All I can remember was that my legs were engulfed in mud as I would stand guard duty, or that I would squat in an outpost reporting the approach of enemy aircraft, unsuccessfully trying to keep warm and to ward off trench foot.

I recall bivouacing at Southhampton, just after we left Kent, waiting to cross the channel for Omaha Beach. It was some weeks after D-Day. I had a conversation with an infantryman, a young man about my age, whose outfit was heading for Normandy. His regiment had just been addressed by an officer who pointed out to the men that casualties could be heavy, that "as many as 50% of you men could be killed or wounded."

"In other words," continued the officer, "the man standing on your left and the man standing on your right probably won't come back."

I shook my head sympathetically as the infantryman related the story.

"I imagine that shook you up," I said.

"Well, it's a funny thing," he said. "Every man standing there looked to the man on his left and then to the man on his his right, and thought 'you poor sonofabitch.' I know that's how I reacted."

Denial is the stuff that heroes are made of, a peculiar mental phenomenon that makes fighting men out of cowards, and I confess one that kept me from clawing my way on my hands and knees toward the boots of an army officer, pleading, "Oh, please, sir, please send me home to my mother."

At no time in Britain or on the continent can I recall any homesickness, any longing to see my mother. It was odd since only a few years earlier I had been unable to make a full week away from her at Camp Matigwa. But it was Anita I longed for, not my mother. In addition, I was totally free of any of the petty concerns that bother me today. Back then, the focus was on staying alive, and nothing more.

From the time I was thirteen and living in Phoenix, Arizona, my mother "kept company" with a man she worked for. It was an unusual arrangement. He was a gentile and a married man. I'll call him Rex Alderdice. Rex, as I remember him, was always kind to me and very polite. He never took sides in any of the arguments I had with my mother, arguments I always lost, either by the volume of her screaming or by the devastating guilt trips she laid on me. But he was very good to her. He was a government bureaucrat, and whenever he was transfered to a different city, he took her with him, and she in turn took me. I was the kid on the end of the conga line. As it turned out, I was a lot closer to Rex than to my own father. That wasn't hard since I never saw my father. Rex, on the other hand, especially during my four years in Phoenix, was around all the time.

Rex was quite a presence in Phoenix. He was tall, and towered over my mother by nearly a foot. A heavy-set man, he wore dark suits and white shirts whose collars seemed a bit too tight and left a red bulge around his neck. Anyone who wore a suit and tie in Phoenix during the mid-1930's had to be treated with respect, if not reverence, and Rex, with his dignified bearing and the grey hair around his temples, was presidential in appearance. When I entered the army, it was reassuring to know that Rex was in the picture. If my mother had been alone, I would have felt that she was focusing entirely on me, depending on me, and that would have been a concern I was happy not to have. It was a familiar story to me. But with Rex around, the pressure was off. She could complain to him all she wanted to, lay off her worries on him. Everything that had previously fallen on my shoulders would now fall on Rex. Rex would take care of her if anything came up. In looking back, my three years of service were a trade off of sorts, a respite from my mother on one hand, offset, on the other, by a host of other hazards.

Time has passed on, and my feelings about my parents have mellowed. They were adults during the Depression and they never really had a chance in life. My mother, dear soul, was never able to draw a winning hand. She had a failed marriage with my father and a relationship with Rex that was doomed from the beginning. My father, a travelling man, was irretrievably lost, a victim of his own vagrant heart who spent his nights on the road playing poker and, as far as I can tell, never drew a winning hand either. Their son, their only child, stood on the brink of destruction one morning in Southhampton, filled with excitement and fear, waiting to cross the channel to Normandy, hoping to beat the odds, something his parents had never been able to do.

As for Rex, I never saw him after I left for the Army. There has been no closure on that segment of my life. I often think about him and the star-crossed relationship he had with my mother all those years, and I wonder how he died and where he is buried. I would pay a visit to his grave if I could find out. But it's doubtful if anyone is around who would know. I still keep a postcard he had written from London during the war, which I received in

Germany. It was addressed to my APO Box and dated May 7, 1945, the day before VE Day. At that time he had a big job with the Office of War Information.

> Dear Melvin:
> Have been here about 30 days and hope to complete and proceed to Paris about June 1. Trust it will be possible to meet you before returning to the States. Should you happen to be in London or Paris during above period please contact me at the OWI office. Your mother writes regularly re her War Bond activities and she is doing a swell job. I hope you are well and trust it won't be too long before you are heading back home. Kind personal regards and best wishes.
>
> R.A.

It was not until September 25, 1944, that our battalion landed at Omaha Beach. We were assigned to the Ninth U.S. Army, Lieutenant General W. H. Simpson in command. By that time, over three months after D-Day, Allied tanks and infantry had pushed the Germans out of Normandy.

Soon after landing, we motor-convoyed through the wreckage of the villages of Normandy. Passing through, I remember being stunned by the devastation, buildings half standing, their sub-structures a breath away from collapse. The scene was as shattering to me as any I had seen in London during the V-1 bombings. When we arrived at the marshalling area at Ste. Mere Eglise, we were now on the edge of the fighting, and not quite in the thick of the action. We remained there for nearly three weeks. My memory, try as I might to jog it, went dead after that time. I know, from Lieutenant White's chronicle, that from Ste. Mere Eglise we dipped south to LeMans, and then proceeded northeast toward Paris, Reims, and finally into Namur and Liege, Belgium.

We arrived at Valkenberg, Holland, in late October, 1944. We stayed in southern Holland (Limborg Province) throughout the winter of 1944-1945, over five months in the same area, caught up in the Battle of the Bulge which began in November of

1944 when the Germans broke through Allied lines creating a bulge in our western line of defense. We engaged low and medium level German aircraft, anywhere from three to three-dozen enemy aircraft a night, throwing up both machine gun and 90mm fire, and occasionally getting strafed by Junker 88's

The exhausted gun crews huddled against the cold in their gun emplacements while Lt. Hillary Garret, Sergeant Frank Allison and I, tried to fend off the murderously cold winter crouched in an observation outpost some miles away.

Some of us were billeted in a little Dutch town called Gulpen, in a small unoccupied farmhouse belonging to Hansen, the local baker, whose shop was just down the road. He had a young daughter, Josephine, a smiling child of 16 or 17, I think, who took a special liking to me. I would see her hanging around the farmhouse, acting very busy, all the while intrigued by the American soldiers. She wore wooden shoes and a Dutch boy cap and looked astonishingly like the illustration on the label of a can of Dutch Boy Cleanser. She did her chores on the family farm and occasionally made bread deliveries on her horse. She was a devout Catholic who was quite aware that I didn't share her religion. I believe, on reflection, that she would have tried to extract a proposal of marriage from me on the spot if I had been a Catholic. This was confirmed many years later when she referred to me in a Maastricht newspaper as the man she would have married had our religions been the same.

The circumstances behind that interview came about because of an essay I had written in 1986 for *The New York Times*. It was called "A Nightingale Sang." In the essay I had contrasted the young women I had met during the war with the young women of today, the latter crimp-faced and seemingly always quarrelsome and bad tempered. I had mentioned Josephine as an example of the loving and tender women of the wartime years. The article fell into the hands of an editor of the Maastricht newpaper, and he promptly launched a promotion to reunite the two of us. Unable at first to locate Josephine, the newspaper then gave the stunt a double-whammy by running a search for her. I was told that hun-

dreds of Dutch Josephines answered the newspaper's advertise-
ment before the right one eventually emerged. The real Josephine
had produced as proof of our friendship a photo taken shortly after
my bar mitzvah. There I was, my young boy's face staring back at
me on the front page of *Der Limborger,* alongside a current picture
of Josephine. She was thin, her gray hair recently washed and set
in apparent anticipation of having her picture taken. Next to her,
my picture made me look like her grandson. When that picture was
taken I was barely 13, an eighth-grade student at the Kenilworth
school in Phoenix, Arizona, posing in front of a palm tree, wearing dirty jeans and a short-sleeve shirt. I have no idea why I had
the snapshot with me, or how I came to give her that particular
one. But she had kept it all those years. It was very touching. But
hadn't I also kept one of her, taken while she was sitting on her
horse? And hadn't I also saved her letters, some written in Dutch,
the later ones, which someone had written for her, in English?

"*Lieve* Melvin," she wrote. "It is already long time since we
heard anything of you. We have had much soldier boys in our
house but I didn't meet such a nice boy as you. I have always
thought of you and I hope you didn't forget me. I forget you
never."

Der Limborger had written me asking me to come to
Maastricht to be re-united with her. Mere puffery. I asked my wife
how she felt about my going. "I think you should go," I remember her saying, "but if you go, don't bother to come back."

Not long ago I received a phone call from Josephine's sister
who was living in Canada. She had recently been to Gulpen to visit
her sister, and had greetings from Josephine. She told me that her
sister had remarried, still hadn't learned to speak English, and was
still chain-smoking. And so the story ends, and no doubt it's just
as well.

My one big brush with death was in Gulpen. It happened one winter night while I was manning the plotting board in the computer,
tracking the whereabouts of enemy aircraft. Lt. White was the officer in charge. It was a moonless night, and only a few aircraft were

in the immediate area. Suddenly, shattering the silence, there came a transmission over the 543 radio warning us that German parachutists were descending over our position. Someone doused the lights in the computer. I automatically reached for my rifle and was putting on my helmet when I was overtaken with a kind of panic that I had never experienced before. The enemy was somewhere out in the darkness, either descending out of the sky or crawling up to our radar installation, machine guns and grenades poised. Get rid of the radar and they render the battery's four 90-mm guns useless. But I wasn't rational enough at the time to think of that. They were after me, only me, and I had no escape. Outside the computer it was so dark it would be impossible to spot anyone to shoot at. There was no clue as to where the chutists might be lurking. I was going to die, and the suspense was agonizing. My breath came in short gasps. I was disoriented. My eyes were open but I was unable to see, unable to focus on my surroundings. At any moment I would be ripped open and blown away. There was no place to hide, and I was choking on my fear. But as quickly as the alert arrived, so did it end. The lights were restored in the computer. I returned to the plotting board and sat there shaking for the rest of my duty.

We were under one kind of stress or another during our three months in Gulpen. The strain of being together, in one place, in bitter cold, and having to endure nightly bombings and strafings, made us edgy and short-tempered. A dozen of us would bed down in sleeping bags on the floor of Hansen's farmhouse. It wasn't unusual to be awakened by someone stepping on your recumbent form on the way to the window to urinate. You could always tell how urine-productive the night was by the number of tell-tale yellow tracks in the snow as well as by the number of arguments over the ruckus created by men on nocturnal piss-call.

Fights were not unusual. It's hard to imagine today that I could have been locked in a struggle to the death with the late Herman Reading, one of my closest pals; or that one of the Mexican guys ("Snake," by nickname, because of his elongated penis) had me pinned to the floor, the point of his bayonet at my throat, his eyes glaring a fiery hatred, until someone mercifully pulled him off me. I had a sick feeling in my stomach for days, but soon Snake and I patched things up. Good old Snake, he never showed up at any of the reunions, and it wasn't until recently that I found out that he was still living.

I often wonder how the conduct of men under battle stress can become so utterly inhuman, but I have seen my buddies pissing on the bodies of dead German soldiers, and for all I know I might have been one of them. I have seen them in acts of mutilating German civilians, of looting farm houses for food and of viciously debasing women to the point where legally it would become rape. I myself have callously exploited the awful plight of German women, hungry for a taste of chocolate, for a cigarette, or for a pair of stockings, and doing it without regard for the moral compromise they evidently had to make. The men I know today are not the same men I knew during the war, and I too am not the same man. But living, as we did, under conditions of fear, cold, filth and debasement, has a way of permitting easy access to whatever beasts lie within us. No, indeed, the close friendship I feel today toward the men with whom I served did not exist then. Our friendships were cultivated over the years as an outgrowth of one momentous experience followed by years of annual reunions. Through the years I've come to know the men better and to respect them more as men. We have a history, we of the 124th. We're an institution, one every bit as sacred to us as the Constitution. We were born under the Wilson, Harding or Coolidge administrations, fought under Roosevelt and Truman. We're so well-seasoned, in fact, that most of us can hardly move around.

So any notion that we entered the war as friends and continued the war as friends would be naive. In many cases the friendships developed later. In the beginning, however, there were such men as Elvin Hardin, Danny Ciccelli, Bruce Brodie, George Duranto, Al Satosanti, Vito Sangervasi, Phil Rodriguez, Herman Reading, Charlie Murchison, Tony Accardo, Claude Walters, George Leach, Paul Poche, Chris Winkler, Joe Murabito, Jim

Oxford, Dee Lemaster, Johnny Keck, Cortez Hunter, and Don Kellog, men with whom I hit it off immediately. Then later in the war, I also counted as my friends Ed Soares, Bill Rizos, Earl White, Don Silva, Ed Singleton, Harold Pilger, and Bob Goss. Our reunions brought in a whole new group of friends, men I either didn't know well or wasn't especially close to during the war. Take the grand old man of the battalion, Ed Harris, and Ysabel Contreras, Hank Stefani, Frank Fratello, John Behl, Jack McCarthy, Ralph Olsen, Bo Smith, Paul Heiser, Huey Long, and others too numerous to list. Some are still living, many have passed away. No matter what, I still see them in my mind's eye as they were in our group photographs, taken in 1943 and 1944, somber, determined and hopeful.

Early in March, 1945, I said goodbye to Josephine, and we convoyed to Koslar, Germany, to protect bridges over the Roer River. From there, we moved to Venlo, Holland, to defend an airfield as well as recently constructed bridges over the Maas River. A week later we moved to Wesel, Germany, to guard the bridge over the Rhine, which the battalion had crossed a day earlier. It was here that we first experienced ground combat, a facet of the war which proved far less to my liking than the artillery.

I acted as a road-guard during the Rhine crossing, directing the battalion convoy over the bridge. I was posted on the east side of the span, and while standing there I suddenly heard sirens and the rumble of a motorcade on the bridge. The air seemed to be supercharged. Presently, I saw several jeeps with 50-calibre machine-guns mounted on the hood, followed by two staff cars with flags on the front fender denoting the rank of the occupants. In this case, the flag had five stars. I was reeling from the excitement but still remembered to salute the vehicle. No sooner had I finished my salute than I saw the open jeep, following close behind the staff car. There were three men seated in the back of the jeep, all wearing overcoats, an army blanket covering each man's lap. They were instantly recognizable. The three were Bernard Montgomery, Winston Churchill and Dwight Eisenhower. They turned in synchronic military precision to return my salute. There I was, a pfc, a nobody out of Phoenix, Des Moines and Chicago, the most inconsequential, insignificant cog in a vast war machine, receiving a salute from among three of the most powerful military men in the world.

But did it really happen? Did I make up the story to impress the men in A Battery, and after the telling and retelling come to believe I had actually seen them. I don't know. No one believed my story at the time, and I can't say I blamed them. When you come right down to it, how ridiculous to think that these three masterminds of the war would be travelling together in a front line position. One mortar, one grenade, a few bursts of rifle fire — any one of those could severely rupture the war effort. But, yet, I can

Home by Christmas. Home by Christmas. That's what the guys are saying. But I (extreme left) have a problem. Where is home, anyway? (Rest stop enroute to Marsielles on our way home, 1945)

see still see them clearly, a picture so real that it will never leave me — Monty, wearing a beret, seated on the left, Churchill, a jowly, pasty-faced old gent, seated in the center, and Ike, wearing his overseas cap, seated on the right. So check me out, you stateside, desk-top military historians. Were they on the Wesel bridge, March 24, 1945, or was it some fabrication of mine or, at worst, an hallucination?

Another time I experienced the same confusion between fantasy and reality. It was shortly before VE-Day. Our battery came upon a compound of Wehrmacht troops in what appeared to be a semi-permanent installation. After we spotted them, we dispersed and cautiously began walking up a small rise anticipating engaging them with grenades and small arms fire. I was paralyzed with fear, as I was most of the time. I was convinced that I was about to die, and just at a time when the German army was in retreat and the war nearly over. Suddenly, to my astonishment, I witnessed a miracle. The Germans, in small groups, began to descend the hill on which they were encamped. They were unarmed, their hands in the air. We didn't exactly capture them, they surrendered. At this point, we became infused with a jolt of machoism, and began rounding up our captives as though we were herding cattle into a pen. While I was busy waving my rifle around, using it to guide and prod the Germans, I was approached by a German officer, a colonel, I believe. He was an impressive figure, tall, erect, a man obviously of good breeding. He wore the Iron Cross First Class.

"Excuse me," he said, speaking in flawless English. "I left my digitalis in the top left hand drawer of my desk in my quarters. I would be obliged if you would bring it to me."

"Your what?" I replied.

"My digitalis. It is medicine for my heart. You'll find it, I'm sure."

I thought for a moment. If I complied with his request I would have felt that I was being ordered around by the enemy. I wouldn't stand still for that. Moreover, he was my captive.

"I'll take your Iron Cross," I said abruptly. It was a demand, not a request.

"Of course," he replied, with unfailing etiquette. Deliberately, he removed the medal and handed it to me. I put it in my pocket and strode back up the rise to the command post. On reflection, it was a foolish thing to do. The desk could have been booby-trapped. There could have been more of the enemy in the command post waiting to blow my head off.

I returned a few moments later with his digitalis. He thanked me curtly. I asked him to go down the hill and join the other prisoners. He was the enemy, the killer of Jews, and yet, as he walked away, I regretted taking his Iron Cross. There needn't have been a *quid pro quo,* for I had destroyed the nobility of my act by asking for the medal. He must have been very proud of it. In his own way, the German officer emerged as more of a gentleman than I did, and over the years I've come to hate him for it. The Iron Cross is in a drawer at home along with other war souvenirs. When I am asked how I got it I tell the story of the colonel and his digitalis. At least I think that's how I got it.

The battalion remained in Wesel for nearly three weeks before moving to Emmern, Germany, to guard bridges over the Weser River. Eventually we moved to Warburg, Germany, where the war ended. I can't recall any celebration on VE Day because most of us feared we'd be shipped to the Pacific theater to fight the Japanese. But on August 15, V-J Day, those fears were allayed. Most of us had accumulated a sufficient number of points (points were calculated to consider time overseas plus battles engaged in) to be shipped home.

Shortly before December, 1945, we left Camp Lucky Strike in Marseilles for the long trip home by Liberty Ship, but not before having received the following commendation from the Commanding General of the Ninth U.S. Army:

TO: All officers and men of the Ninth U.S. Army.

1. In your advance through Germany you have added a glorious chapter to military history and contributed in large measure to the crushing defeat of the German army.

Significant milestones in that advance were the operations in the Western Rhineland, the crossing of the Roer River, the crossing of the Rhine, the reduction of the northern half of the Rhur Pocket, and the dash across northern Germany to the Elbe.

2. In your last great operation east of the Rhine your exploits will rank among the greatest of military achievements. To list only a few of your outstanding achievements I cite the juncture with our brothers-in-arms of the First Army; your making contact with our Russian allies; your capture of more than 519,000 members of the Wermacht; your liberation of nearly 350,000 Allied prisoners of war and nearly 631,000 citizens of subjugated nations; your capture of more than 3500 cities, towns and villages and some 11,340 square miles of Germany. In destroying German Army Group Northwest and Eleventh German Army, and forcing the surrender of both the Ninth and Twelfth German Armies, you delivered a vital blow against hostile resistance in Northern Germany.

3. My congratulations to each and every officer and man upon your brilliant accomplishments and my heartfelt thanks for your never-failing support. Command of the Ninth Army I consider a great privilege; service in it, along with you, is a great honor.

W.H. Simpson
Lieutenant General, U. S. Army
Commanding

SIX

While in Scottsdale, my thoughts turned to Phil Rodriguez. He had passed away about a year before I saw his name on the list of the deceased. Phil and I went back a long way together. As a matter of fact we had arrived at Camp Callan for basic training on the same day early in 1943. He was a Mexican from Montebello, California, a cocky guy, as I remembered him back then, with his Indian heritage written all over his mongrel face. We were just kids, barely 18, and wary of each other at first, as you might expect, but eventually we forged a friendship that went on for the next 53 years.

We were a mis-matched pair in every way — Phil had never known a Jew, and I had never known a Mexican. We had been thrown together in a big melting pot of an army camp where soldiers from every imaginable background reported for duty sporting their spanking new uniforms, and along with them a slew of home-earned prejudices. For me, alone and hard-pressed for a buddy, even a casual acquaintance like Phil meant a great deal to me.

Phil, however, fell short of being the ideal pal. To this day, I can't think of a thing we had in common. Actually, if I dare admit it, I was a little ashamed to be seen with him. He was uneducated and rowdy and only semi-literate. I preferred hanging around with Bruce Brodie, Charlie Murchison, Herman Reading or Danny Cicchelli. With Bruce and Charlie, especially, I could talk about books and popular music because by this time I had already read such writers as Thomas Wolfe, John Dos Passos and Hemingway, and in addition, like my friend, Don Marks, I knew the words to every popular song written since 1937.

There was a strong sense of refinement in my family, even though my mother and I were poor and forced to reside with relatives. My aunt, with whom we lived, had moved to California with her sister shortly after the war ended. They lived in Los Angeles at the Gaylord Hotel on Wilshire Boulevard, and in their years together would sooner die than enter a restaurant that didn't have white linen tableclothes and napkins. My mother, too, even though she supported us with menial clerical jobs, would rather cross the street than have to pass people like Phil whom she would perceive as riff-raff.

Nothing that Phil enjoyed doing was of any interest to me, and that put the two of us at odds from the very beginning. When

He was a street kid from the Mexican ghetto. I was a Jew reared in a kosher household on Des Moines's northside, itself a ghetto. But in spite of our differences we had one of those rare friendships that never could have sustained itself without the poignant memories of our years together in the Army.

he had an evening pass he would head for some of the dives off the base where he would drink, fight and raise hell, often staggering back to the barracks, weaving drunkenly toward his cot. Don't get the idea that I was an angel, but when I had the money and a pass, I went in for tamer pursuits. I liked hitch-hiking into LaJolla with Charlie Murchison for dinner at the Valencia Hotel. Not only was the food good but the table linens were gleaming white and the silverware was polished to a high gloss.

Phil and I went on to fight in the European theater in 1944 and 1945 and, along with the rest of the outfit, were finally disbanded at Chiem See, Germany, August 15, 1945. I was shipped home three months later, there to resume my life at peace with the circle of boyhood friends I'd left behind. Or so I thought at the time.

I was sure that there was no man in the battalion I would miss seeing again, not even Phil. But life is not so predictable. In 1949, within four years of our discharges, many of the men in the battalion discovered that they missed the old outfit, and I, the outcast, oddly enough, was the one who missed it the most. What I didn't realize at the time was that the relationships that were formed during the war could not be shut off just because the war itself had ended. The shared experiences of combat were too strong, too binding.

A few years before he died, I visited Phil in Montebello. He lived in a small unimposing house on Olympic Boulevard. His five sons had grown up in that house, and their framed pictures, each in a Marine uniform, hung on a living room wall surrounding a flag-draped photograph of Phil and his wife, Lupe, taken during Phil's early days in the army. A crucifix was mounted above the assembly of photographs, and the wall itself seemed to serve as a shrine for their worship of God, family and country. I have run across many self-described patriots over the years, the loud-mouth super patriots and the slick professionals both, but never one with the simple dignity and quiet dedication of Philip Rodriguez.

The photograph of Phil and Lupe, taken while we were stationed in the states, portrayed a smiling young couple, her cheek pressed against his, she a plain young woman with swept-back brown hair, dark eyes and fair skin. Phil, in contrast, was the dark-skinned, street kid, wearing a non-issue garrison cap tilted jauntily to one side. His uniform was barren of medals except for a sharp-shooters medal on his chest and a gold "U.S." and gold artillery insignia pinned to the lapels of his Eisenhower jacket.

Phil and I saw plenty of action, and we both lived to tell about it. But it was the Viet Nam war that Phil couldn't escape from. One son, Reggie, a Marine, was killed in Nam. His eldest son, Frank, also a Marine, was wounded there and later died of his wounds in the states. Two other sons, Anthony and Phil, are serving in the Marines. John, another son, is an ex-Marine gunnery sergeant, having served in the Far East. If all that was not a sufficient patriotic sacrifice, Phil lost a brother at Iwo Jima.

Phil's second eldest, John, had married a Japanese woman while stationed in Japan, and the couple had twin boys, Joe and Ray, whose mixed ancestry is visible at a glance. John's wife had refused to come to America, and the couple was subsequently divorced, the boys then coming to live in Montebello. Handsome, studious and well-behaved, the boys have been brought up by Phil and Lupe and attend school in Montebello.

Phil and his wife had been married over fifty years. He retired in his early 60's after having worked for the Los Angeles Department of Water and Power for 36 years. Later he suffered a stroke leaving him temporarily paralyzed on his left side. But his recovery had been so remarkable that there was no visible damage to his body.

"I feel great," he said, "I'm ashamed to feel so good."

"Enjoy it while you can," I told him at the time. "The years have a way of catching up with you."

"The hell with that — you and me, we're going to live forever," said Phil.

The three of us were sitting in his living room. Their grandsons, Joe and Ray, were doing homework in a back room. Lupe, stocky and energetic, talked about her recent knee replacement surgery performed at a local hospital. The operation was not successful, and she and Phil have consulted another surgeon in whom they have confidence, but they are short of funds. She had a rapid-fire speech pattern, and described her knee problems in a stream of words that rolled off her tongue in salvos.

Money problems had also made it difficult for Phil to attend reunions. He never asked for any help, but when one of the men would extend it he accepted graciously, and no further word was said. Along with a few others, I was one of his benefactors, but it was Ed Harris, who has since passed away, who made the biggest sacrifice for Phil. Ed would drive miles out of his way from his home in LaCanada, California, to pick up Phil and drive him to Vancouver, Washington, to Las Vegas, Reno, Phoenix or wherever a reunion was being held, and then return him to his front door in Montebello.

It was getting on toward lunchtime. I said goodbye to Lupe, and Phil and I strolled over to Jimmy's Family Restaurant at 7th and Whittier Boulevard. It was a comfortable coffee shop. From the look of the place I assumed it was Greek-owned. While Phil and I were eating, a heavy-set man, an Anglo, stopped by our table. He was Montebello's chief of police, Steve Simarian.

"How's the boss?" he asked Phil.

Phil said she was doing great, and then introduced me as an old army buddy who had come to visit. We shook hands.

"Don't let him fool you," the chief said to me, smiling. "Lupe is the real hero in the family."

Before he left, the chief reached over and grabbed our check. I started to protest.

"Forget it," Phil said, "the cops always get their way."

It was then that I became aware of just how beloved Phil and Lupe were in Montebello. They had been there all their lives — law-abiding, respected and loved in this community of 40,000 just east of Los Angeles. I suddenly realized how much I was enjoying myself. I felt serene, insulated from worry. There I was in Montebello, in a pleasant restaurant on a warm January afternoon, surrounded by pretty waitresses, by Phil, my brother-in-arms, and by a good guy named Steve Simarian.

Phil and I traded recollections for awhile, but he suddenly paused and leaned toward me.

"If you have time, there's something I want to show you."

"If I have time? That's all I do have."

"Let's walk back to the house and get your car," he said. "It's a short drive."

Along the way, I asked him how he was spending his time. Was he ever lonely? Did he feel depressed? — all the dark feelings that had been expressed time and again by so many others in the battalion.

"Oh, sure, I get feeling low lots of times, but then I go out and exercise, and that helps. But there are times," he added, "when even that doesn't help."

"Same here," I said, "but what are we going to do when we can't exercise anymore?"

"Who knows? Just keep busy. Lupe and I drive to Vegas a couple of times a month. We have a hell of a time there. I guess we'll keep doing that."

"That's not all bad."

"Far from it," he said. "And of course we take care of Joe and Ray. That keeps us real busy. I take them to school every day, and then pick them up in the afternoon. Their school is only a block away, but I want to do it. Nowadays you have to."

"I was about to ask you if you thought times were better when we got out of the army than they are now, but you already answered that."

"There's no comparison," said Phil. "All my kids went to the same school. I never took them and never picked them up. We never worried about them. Times were much better then."

We got into my car, and I started the engine.

"Where we heading?"

"I want you to see the park the city named after Reggie."

"You're kidding," I said in disbelief.

"No," he said, "it's true. You'll see."

We drove several blocks to a large park, several acres in size. As we approached, I saw a large rustic sign reading "Reggie Rodriguez Park, City of Montebello." There were two plaques set in concrete at the base of the sign, dedicating the park to the memory of Marine Lance Corporal Reginald Rodriguez. Phil and I stood silently. Off in the distance, several youths stood around smoking, a boom-box blaring. As I stared down at the plaques, I noticed some cigarette paper on the ground, the kind used for rolling marijuana cigarettes, in front of the plaques honoring the memory of Phil's son. Phil had noticed it, too. I expected him to say something, but he said nothing.

"Damnit," I said angrily. I kicked the cigarette paper away with my foot.

Phil seemingly felt no anger. He merely shrugged. He was past all the hurt, and no longer seemed to care.

"We didn't have this junk when we were in the army," I said. He smiled.

"We probably wouldn't have won the war if we did," he said.

We stood together quietly, neither of us speaking.

"Philip," I said, finally, "do you have any idea why guys like us keep coming back to reunions?"

He bent down to pick up the litter in front of the plaques and pondered my question.

"Well, I'm not exactly sure, but the 124th is important to me. I love all you guys. I guess I'll keep going as long as we have them."

"I feel the same way, but I wonder if loving the guys is the whole answer."

"What do you mean?"

"I don't know for sure," I said, "but I think it's about survival, too."

"Survival?"

"Yep."

"You mean like staying alive?"

"Look, Phil, I think we feel, somewhere inside us, that if the battalion survives, each of us, you and me and all the guys who show up for the reunions, are going to survive, too. And if we don't show up then the battalion will fall apart, it'll die, and all of us will die right along with it."

"So you're telling me that the battalion is our life. Right?"

"Right, the blood of our blood."

"But the outfit broke up in 1945," he said. "It's dead. Deader than hell. There's nothing left but a few old guys like us."

"Yeah, but those of us left have this bond, see? Nothing's stronger than that bond, Phil. What forged it is the miserable war we fought together. Take away the reunions and you take away the battalion, and those of us left won't have a thing in our lives to replace it with."

I placed my arm on his shoulder and looked him in the eye. I continued talking.

"You talked about the battalion being dead, Phil. But when you come down to it so are we, you and me. We died a long time ago, and that's the truth. We don't work; we draw social security. All we do is take up space and drive ourselves crazy looking for something to keep busy."

"C'mon,"

"It's true, but at our reunions, for three lousy days a year, we rise from the grave and become something special — not to the rest of the world but to ourselves. In short, old friend, we live again."

We stood on the sidewalk in front of his home. It was time for me to get on the freeway and head back to L.A.

We shook hands, and then, as we have done for years, embraced each other, almost as if we were afraid to let go.

"Goodbye, Phil," I said.

As I turned to leave, he called after me.

"Hey, watch that. We don't say goodbye, we say 'see you later.'"

Not long ago I received a phone call from Lupe. I heard the sadness in her voice almost immediately. Something was wrong.

"Phil passed away," she told me, struggling to get the words out. "He went very fast. He always talked about you, Mel. I wanted to call you."

"Damnit, Lupe. How did it happen?"

"He got up in the morning and did his exercises. He said he wanted to take a nap. He always took his nap after lunch. It wasn't like him to take his nap after breakfast. He always talked about you, Mel."

"Then what happened, I mean after he took his nap?"

"I could tell he was sick," she said, speaking very rapidly. "I called 9-1-1. Pretty soon the paramedics came. They gave him a shot and pounded on his chest but they couldn't bring him to. The ambulance came. They took him to the hospital. He never came to. He died ten minutes later. They couldn't do anything."

"I'm sorry, Lupe."

"He always talked about you. He went very fast."

"When is the funeral?"

She continued speaking rapidly, her words, spoken with a slight Mexican accent, poured forth in a confusing stream. She gave me the name of the mortuary. Moritz Funeral Home in Montebello. I told her I'd come out if I could get on a plane in time. She neither encouraged nor attempted to disuade me.

"I'll do the best I can," I said.

After I rang off I called the funeral home. A lady filled me in on the details. It was now Tuesday afternon. A viewing of the body Wednesday afternoon... a Rosary that evening at St. Benedict's...a Mass Thursday morning at St.Benedict's...a processional to Resurrection cemetery after Mass. It would have to be a quick trip, no chance of attending Mass Thursday morning. My wife and I were leaving for a week's vacation on Friday. I could make it, but barely. I considered not going but that would have meant not seeing Phil that one last time, even in a state of repose.

The flight to L.A. was long, six and a half hours, two stops. I rented a car, checked into a hotel near the airport, then tackled the 45 mile freeway trip to Montebello.

Montebello is a well-kept, predominantly Hispanic community along the Whittier Boulevard corridor between Monterey

Park and the city of Whittier, and getting there is not easy for someone who isn't used to the L.A. freeway system. You first have to fight your way through downtown L.A. with its maze of criss-crossing freeways, each bound for different destinations in different directions. — the Harbor, the Hollywood, the San Bernardino, the Santa Ana, the Pasadena and the Pomona. No matter how many times I've driven through the gray industrial thicket of east L.A., the journey never gets easier. The eyes spin in their sockets, the head aches, the nerves jangle. I finally sailed east on the Pomona freeway until I reached Montebello. I found the mortuary nestled among the small shops and cafes of Whittier boulevard. It was located only a few blocks from St. Benedict's. I sense that an entire life could be spent on Whittier Boulevard without the need to venture beyond its borders.

The mortuary's parking lot was not filled. Standing outside the mortuary were Joey and Ray, John Rodriguez's two sons, whom I had met the last time I visited Phil. They didn't recognize me. Both wore glasses, the lenses large and round, the frames dark. With their mixed Mexican-Japanese ancestry both boys looked like miniature Mr. Motos.

I entered the mortuary. Sitting in the foyer were several Mexican women, mostly young, heavy set. They were chatting amiably. Once inside the visitation room, I walked toward the open casket. Chairs were lined up auditorium style. A few elderly Mexican men sat quietly in the center of the room. An old lady, her head enshrouded in a black shawl, sat alone at the rear of the room, head bowed, quietly praying. At the casket, I took a long last look at Phil. I was appalled at what I saw. He was dressed in a colorful long-sleeved shirt covered with Indian designs, set off by a bolo tie with a turquoise lanyard. A silver buckle with a turquoise stone adorned his belt. His hands clutched his rosary beads. I had never before seen Phil in Indian clothing or wearing Indian jewelry. He had always dressed in casual American-style clothing or, when he appeared at our reunion banquets, in a conventional suit and tie. It was apparent that Phil had Indian blood but seeing him dressed that way in the coffin made him seem like a stranger. I was tempted to bend down and kiss my old friend on his forehead, but seeing all the mortuary war paint on his face only served to point up the differences between us, differences that had long been forgotten, until this moment.

All of a sudden, I wasn't happy about having travelled all the way to California only to find Phil lying in his coffin, all done up and powdered and rouged and looking like a wax likeness of Cochise. This was not Phil lying in front of me, not the sweet man I joked with and shared Calvados with during the winter of 1945. But I had to see him this one last time, if only to fix his face permanently in my mind.

It was something I had failed to do with my friend, Danny Cicchelli. Danny had come to Chicago from his home in Detroit for his niece's June graduation. It was late in the evening when he called, and he wanted to meet me at a restaurant. I told him no; it was too late, I said, and besides I would see him a few months later at our reunion in September. That summer he died. He was loud, combative and profane, and a good friend. But which of his faces do I place in the locket of my mind — Danny with the long scar running down the side of his face. Or Danny flicking the tip of his thumb from between his teeth in a gesture of reprisal directed to the back of Sergeant Snopek. Or Danny, that time on Louisiana manuevers, when he straightened my pack and held some of its weight with his free hand as we marched. I'm missing that single clear picture of him. I would have had it if I hadn't passed up seeing him in Chicago. I wanted to make sure it wouldn't happen in Phil's case.

There was no sign of Lupe. I walked outside the mortuary. There were now more visitors than when I had first arrived. I spotted a tall, strapping Mexican, smiling and chatting casually with some of the visitors. He resembled Phil in every way except for the Indian features. As I approached him he took only brief notice of me and continued talking to the other visitors. I interrupted him and introduced myself as an army friend of his father's. He took that news matter-of-factly, and it was evident he had never heard my name. He told me he was John Rodriguez, the eldest son. He was a retired Marine gunnery sergeant who had fought in Viet Nam. He was 51, the father of Joey and Ray, and he lived in Aurora, Colorado. I knew a lot about him from my previous visit with Phil, his multiple marriages, his divorce from his Japanese wife, his two sons who were cared for by Lupe and Phil. We conversed for a few moments, but he neglected to introduce me to any of the other visitors milling about, and exhibited no interest in my relationship with Phil or in why I had come to California for the funeral. When I asked where his mother was, he told me she was off running errands and would be back shortly. I told him I'd wait around, extended my condolences and walked off.

I sat down on a bench outside the mortuary. I was an Anglo among all the Mexicans, dressed up in suit and tie and looking out-of-place, and yet no one introduced themselves or showed any curiosity about my presence. Except for one man. Seated on the bench next to me was a burly middle-aged Mexican. I began chatting with him. He introduced himself as Ron Orozco, an old friend of Reggie Rodriguez, Phil and Lupe's son who was killed in Nam. He pointed to a young man in the crowd, whom I would have judged to be 21 or 22. He was Reggie Rodriguez, Jr. I was startled to learn that Phil's late son had himself been the father of a son, now a handsome well-dressed young man. It made Nam seem so long ago, as though I had been lost in a time warp.

On a recent visit to Washington I had visited the Viet Nam memorial. There, engraved in the marble was the name of Marine Corporal Reggie Rodriguez. I recall having sent a pencil tracing of his name to Phil and Lupe, imagining all the time that the man whose name I had traced was, even at that time, still a fresh faced young man.

Ron Orozco had a full black beard and walked with a cane. I noticed that his right hand was misshapen. He had one eye. His injuries had been sustained at Nam, where he had received massive shrapnel injuries. He was a gentle, patient man who explained what a Rosary was and gave me additional information about the following day's events. The mass was to begin the following morning at 10:30 and since I was on an early afternoon flight out of LAX,

I wouldn't have time to attend.

Finally, I spotted Lupe just before 5 pm when the mortuary was about to close. She was in the center of a group of friends who had come to view Phil's body. As I walked toward her, she recognized me immediately. I hugged her and told her how sorry I was about Phil. She asked me if I had viewed the body. I told her I had. Nevertheless, she guided me back inside the mortuary and together we walked over to the casket, passing the same old men seated away from the casket and the old lady praying at the rear of the auditorium.

"Doesn't Philip look wonderful," she said, proudly.

"Yes he does, Lupe," I lied. "He looks very lifelike."

"My little Indian," she said plaintively.

"I was surprised to find that you put Indian clothing on him."

"Oh, Phil belonged to the San Gabriel tribe. He had a lot of Indian blood."

"I guess I never realized how much.

"Oh, yes, Phil was an Indian."

"Whatever he was, Lupe, he was my good friend."

"He always talked about you, Mel."

"Well, I'll miss him."

She told me she had to gather up Joey and Ray and take them back home for dinner.

"You're coming to the Rosary, aren't you?"

"Of course," I said.

I was hoping she would invite me back to her home, but the invitation didn't come.

It was shortly after 5 pm and I had nearly two hours to kill. I hadn't the slightest notion of how to use up the time. I started driving east on Whittier Boulevard, looking for a place to sit down and have a drink. I passed from one small town to another, each bearing a Spanish name, but there were no cocktail lounges, only one cheap Mexican cafe after another, each advertising the same specialties — Tacos, Burritos, Tamales, Chili Rellenos, enough visual spiciness to make my stomach growl and my eyes cry out for water.

I found a saloon shortly before I reached the city of Whittier and ordered a vodka. The barmaid shoved the drink and a bowl of popcorn in front of me. I watched a young couple shooting pool for a few minutes, the boy wearing his baseball cap backwards. Then, tiring of the whole scene, I asked the barmaid if she knew a good restaurant. She said her mother worked in a swell place on Rosemead Boulevard. "Have you eaten there?" I asked. "No, but my mother told me the food was good." I took her directions but decided not to stop. Rosemead Boulevard looked like a big traffic hassle so I continued west along Whittier Boulevard, back toward Montebello. When I reached 7th and Whittier, I spotted the place where Phil and I had lunch a few years earlier. Jimmy's Restaurant. I thought about the good time I'd had with Phil. I recalled Steve Simarian, the Montebello police chief, who bought our lunch, and the pretty waitresses in their short skirts. It was as if I had come home. Life could be good after all, and I no longer felt quite as lonely.

There were only a few couples in the restaurant. I took a seat at the counter, and the prettier of the two Hispanic waitresses took my order. After a while, I saw Jimmy heading toward the cash register. There was no doubt that it was he. He was a short, swarthy man with a thick mane of gray hair. The Rosary would be starting soon. I finished eating and took my check to the register. I greeted him with the few words of Greek I knew. He asked me if I was speaking Greek to him. I knew then that I had made a mistake.

"I'm not Greek," he said, cordially. He spoke with a slight middle-eastern accent.

"I'm sorry," I said, "I sort of figured you were."

"Lots of people do, but I'm Iranian."

I introduced myself as a friend of Phil Rodriquez.

"We served in the army together," I explained.

"Did you come in for the mass?"

"Well, not the mass, just the Rosary tonight."

I was surprised that he already knew about Phil.

"Too bad about Phil. I've know Phil and Lupe for a long

time," he said.

"He brought me here for lunch a few years ago. I didn't have a chance to meet you then."

We shook hands.

"My daughter and I are going to the Rosary in a few minutes. I'll see you over there."

"A pleasure meeting you, Jimmy."

"Same here," he said.

I was hoping he'd ask me to join them.

I caught a glimpse of him at St.Benedict's. He was seated in one of the rear rows, just as I was. No one spoke or nodded to me when I walked in. The church was a huge, hollow structure, and all the pews were gradually filling up as I sat and watched the Mexicans genuflect and make the sign of the cross. Finally, when the priest began to speak, his words came out as unfeeling, as hollow as the church itself. I saw no tears, and heard only the impersonal voice of the priest. It was as though all emotion had been snuffed out by the organized ritual of the service and by that huge warehouse of a church. I longed to hear the tearful wail of *Kaddish*, the Jewish prayer for the dead.

At that moment I was suddenly confronted by an unmistakable truth: I had expected to be accepted into Phil's world merely because I had attended his funeral. It was the delusion of an outsider. And yet, in contradiction, it was I who had once turned away from Phil because I didn't consider him my equal. The truth is — I didn't belong to his world any more than he belonged to mine. Neither of us, no matter how intense the yearning, could push his way into the alien world of the other. Different people have different ways. It was best that I left it at that. He was a Mexican, a street-kid from the Mexican ghetto. I was a Jew, reared in a kosher household on Des Moines's northside, itself a ghetto. But in spite of our differences, we had one of those rare friendships, borne out of the loneliness and terror of war, that could never have sustained itself without those poignant memories of our years together in the army. Phil was gone and a piece of the battalion, and a piece of me as well, had gone with him.

I stuck around at the Rosary for half an hour before I walked out.

As I headed back to my car, I thought of Phil's parting words to me a few years before.

"We don't say goodbye," he had said. "We say, 'see you later.'"

I turned around and looked up at St.Benedict's, its huge spire outlined against the darkening sky. Inside lay the body of a fallen comrade dressed up in Indian clothes. That man and I had huddled together to ward off the cold during the winter of 1945. We had swallowed the mud of Holland during nightly strafings by JU 88's and had shivered in a frenzy of fear as German paratroopers descended in the darkness over our position near Wesel, Germany.

"See you later, Phil," I yelled out in the direction of the church.

SEVEN

I often wonder about my attachment to the men I served with during the war. I offer up all sorts of reasons for it. To be sure, there's the unforgettable experience of the war which bonded us together, and there's also the fact that as an only child I craved the presence of siblings in my life — maybe not 750 of them at one time, but at the very least a few I could regard as brothers. As in many families, you want to see your siblings every so often, more often than once a year at reunions. That's why I decided to visit Phil Rodriguez that time before he died, and why, as part of the same swing through some of the western states, I had called on Jim Oxford, Charlie Murchison, Dean Calico, Huey Long, Cortez Hunter, Earl White, Pancho Contreras and John Behl. It wasn't only to interview them for a book. The book was a longshot that might or might not ever come about.

After I visited Phil in Montebello, I went to see Jim Oxford, a rangy soft spoken man in his mid-seventies. He lives alone in Oxnard, California, just north of Los Angeles. During the war we didn't have much to do with each other, and thinking back on the three years we spent together, I have a hard time recalling a time when we exchanged more than a few words. Jim was an ammo loader, a corporal, on one of the gun crews, so he and I were not thrown in with each other on any regular basis. When we were not on duty, I didn't seek him out nor did he have much to do with me. We didn't seem to have anything in common. He was tough-looking and slow talking, a man of few words and great physical strength. He had entered service from his home in Oklahoma.

I was always a little afraid of him. He was a pretty heavy drinker, I knew, and could get wild at times, so at 120 pounds I figured it best to give Jim a wide berth. As it later turned out, I needn't have.

After the army, at our earlier reunions, we saw each other frequently, exchanged some brief pleasantries and went our separate ways. But as the years went by Jim mellowed a great deal. He has become more reserved, more withdrawn, and has an air of gentleness that enables me to feel comfortable in his presence.

His usual attire is western — cowboy hat, boots and western style shirts and jeans. Tall and slender, he strongly resembles Gary Cooper right down to his slow-talking ways. But it is the face where the Cooper resemblance falls apart. Jim's bears the imprint of years of hard physical labor and a well-travelled but rocky life.

At our fiftieth reunion banquet he sat at the table with Bo Smith, Phil Rodriguez, Doreen Harris and me. He was seated immediately to my left. On this night, the high point of the reunion, he wore a blue suit, white shirt, and tie, instead of his usual western clothing. From time to time he left the table for the foyer where the cash bar had been set up — not for a drink because he had quit drinking years before, but to smoke a cigarette. There were ashtrays at each table, and while others smoked freely at their tables, Jim would not. He didn't ask us if we would mind if he smoked, he was simply too polite, too well-mannered, to even pose the question, for that might have proved embarrassing for anyone who would object. Then and there, I was no longer intimidated by Jim Oxford. We were both too old, and anyway I saw him for the first time as the polite, considerate man he really was. What a remarkable discovery: fifty years later I concluded that I genuinely liked him.

I called him after I arrived in L.A. and we arranged to meet at a Baker's Square eatery in Oxnard, just off the Ventura Freeway. I drove up 405, cutting through the mountains, and then headed west on the Freeway, following the Santa Monica mountains, until I reached the Oxnard cutoff. He was waiting for me outside the restaurant, wearing his usual western garb, and looking like Seldom-Seen Slim, the Death Valley Loner. We shook hands, and Jim flicked his cigarette into the parking lot. Once inside the restaurant, the hostess asked if we preferred a smoking or non-smoking table, and I quickly responded 'smoking,' figuring I could be just as deferential to him as he had been to me.

We talked for a few minutes, but he didn't seem overly-interested in the fact that I was writing a book about the battalion. I don't think he attached any more significance to my coming to see him than if it were merely a routine visit between two old vets.

Jim told me he never returned to his home state of Oklahoma after he left the army. The same decision, I knew, had been made by others in the battalion who, once they had left their home states and became exposed to California, found it had drawn them into its web of magic, just as it had for me. The others became transplants, Jim to Oxnard, some to Santa Rosa, Los Gatos and various

When the old timers like us pass on, who will be left to carry on the folkways of the past, a time when you could light up a Camel and enjoy it and be content to take your meals alone in a greasy spoon. Most likely no one.

other communities up and down the coast. But not so with me. I returned to Chicago and my mother, never thinking I had a choice in the matter. But for so many of my buddies, it was clearly a case of "how you going to keep 'em down on the farm after they've seen Paree."

His first job upon leaving the army, he said, was spraying lemon trees for eighty-one cents an hour. Since then he has worked at a variety of jobs — as a diesel mechanic, a welder, a maintenance merchanic. He had quit school after the eighth grade.

He told me he had worked on a construction job in Barstow, California in 1968. He mentioned Barstow because he knew the town had special meaning to the 124th, for at the time it was the closest town of any size to Camp Irwin, where we had trained. As we were having lunch, my mind drifted back to Barstow where an evening pass from Irwin was an excursion into the depths of boredom. The town was then a way-station between Los Angeles and Palm Springs, and everything it had to offer was confined to one street. There was nothing to do but hang out, drink beer and watch gas being pumped, the only business establishments being gas stations, places to eat, and saloons. Once I saw the actor, Frank Morgan, who was passing through, coming out of a restaurant, a good looking woman on his arm. He wore Hollywood-style clothing and walked with an air of joviality and importance, conscious of me and a few other servicemen staring at him. To me, a lonely private hanging out on a dusty street, he made the whole town glitter. He was a celebrity, a star, one of the first ones I had ever seen in person. I can't watch *The Wizard of Oz* today without thinking of the actor and Barstow and the one-horse joint he stepped out of.

I drove through Barstow a few days after I met with Jim. Fifty-one years had gone by since I was last there. The town was spread out and ugly with a huge Hispanic population. It was totally unrecognizable. And yet, even though I realized that he must have died years before, I kept hoping I might catch a glimpse of the Wizard somewhere on the dusty streets.

Jim lives alone. His wife of 50 years died in 1993. Generally, he is not too forthcoming about his personal life, but he mentioned that his mother, then 93, was still alive and living in Bakersfield. He has four brothers and sisters, two others had died.

He is presently wrestling with what to do with his wife's belongings.

"Her baking stuff meant a lot to her," he said, sadly. "It's hard going through her things,"

"What kinds of things?" I asked him.

"All her baking utensils," he said, "they meant a lot to her. She baked and decorated cakes for everybody, all her friends. Birthdays, weddings, that kind of thing. She was very proud of her baking. Some day I'll go through them and give them away. I wouldn't sell them but I'd give them to someone who'd appreciate them."

"That may be harder than you think these days," I said.

He nodded.

"What else, Jim? What are you doing to keep busy?" I asked. "Are you doing any kind of work?"

"Nothing special," he said, "an odd construction job now and then. Mostly, I'm remodeling the house. I started it while my wife was alive. She was the one who wanted it done. I guess I'll just go ahead and finish it up."

As we chatted, I mentioned that I myself would have a tough time living alone, as he does, especially come mealtime.

"Do you cook your own meals?"

"Naw," he said, "I eat out. It gives me a chance to get out of the house. It's something to do."

I had a vision of this tall cowboy ambling up to the counter in any number of greasy spoons, keeping to himself, puffing away on his Camels. I would be doing the same thing, I thought, because that kind of life was perversely appealing to me in these days of loud yuppies nibbling away on goat cheese in trendy restaurants. I found myself thinking of Carl Hubbell, the great New York Giants pitcher in the late 1930's. In his later years, Hubbell was taking his meals alone in a small restaurant in Tempe,

Arizona, where he lived. He was receiving a small pension from Horace Stoneham, his former boss, as repayment for his loyalty to the Giants organization. Hubbell, like so many other baseball greats of the past, cared very little about money but a hell of a lot more about playing baseball, and, as the story has it, would return his annual contract to Stoneham with a note telling his boss to fill in the salary amount and he would sign it. Jim struck me as the same kind of guy. There are still some of us around, men who grew up during the Depression, contented with their lot, aspiring to neither fame nor fortune. Their thinking, which seems to have grown up out of an older culture, has not changed. It is simply this: just let me alone and let me do my thing and give me enough to get by on. When the old timers like us pass on, who will be left to carry on the folkways of the past, a time when you could light up a Camel and enjoy it and be content to take your meals alone in a greasy spoon. Most likely no one.

From the time I went in the army until the early 1970's, nothing gave me more pleasure than cigarettes. They gave me a sense of well-being, soothed my nerves, and helped me think clearly. They consoled me when I was sad and shared my elation in moments of joy. I reached for my early morning cigarette long before reaching out for my wife. They were my constant companions over a cup of coffee and enhanced the enjoyment of a martini in gin joints in most of the civilized world. But above and beyond all this, the seven packs of fags alloted weekly to every soldier in combat helped me survive the war. Addictive or not, who cared? There were far worse things that could happen to you during the war than a mere cigarette addiction. In World War I, apparently a more tedious war than the one I knew, cigarettes were even more indispensable. Because our troops spent anxious days in trenches without a cigarette, it prompted "Black Jack" Pershing to send an urgent message to President Wilson, requesting weekly rations of cigarettes for the men. That no doubt was the forerunner for the stipends we received in the Second World War. Some of us eventually broke up with our long-standing "friends," but not Jim Oxford. He's not one to turn his back on a "friend," and in a way I envy him all the pleasure he continues to receive. But if I had to make the choice all over again I wouldn't have changed my decision. I still would have given them up. Who needs "friends" anyway, especially those who can make you so happy one moment and then abruptly turn on you.

Any discussion of reunions inevitably comes down to recollections of Ed Harris. Although others first came up with the idea — Ed Soares, Tony Rodrigues and a few other men from northern California — it was Ed Harris, the granddaddy of the 124th, who was the leader and the inspiration for all subsequent reunions. He was the spearhead, a man so obsessed with locating all the men, bringing them together year after year, and then making sure, come hell or high water, that they showed up at the reunions, that our annual get-togethers would surely have petered out years before were it not for his efforts. He was our very own *Mr. Keene, Tracer of Lost Persons.* His death a few years ago was a major loss but thus far it hasn't put a serious crimp in reunion turnouts, above and beyond what time itself has accomplished.

Ed was so reunion happy, Jim recalled, that he'd go anywhere to see a buddy, even to the point of showing up at a man's place of work.

"So what's it all about, Jim?" I asked him. I can't figure these reunions. Is it all Ed's doing? Or would we have had them even if Ed hadn't been around?"

He shrugged.

"I'm not sure," he said.

"Well, we're still having reunions even though Ed isn't around anymore."

"That's true," he said.

"Why are we meeting so often while other outfits lost touch with each other long ago? Do you know the answer to that one?"

"Not exactly," he said. "We sure didn't get along all that well during the war."

"I sure as hell didn't," I said.

"The guys I got along with best," he said, "were the little Mexican guys. They used to come looking for me to help them out when they were drunk and got in a fight."

"One of the Mexican guys pulled his bayonet on me once," I said."

"That'll happen," he said. "They've got short tempers."
I nodded vigorously, recalling the episode with "Snake" and the week-long tremors that followed.

"I guess what it comes down to," Jim said, "is that we were like squabbling kids in a family, but we were a family. Yeah, one damn family, that's what the 124th is."

"That about sums it up," I said.

He asked me who else I was going to talk to while I was in California.

"I'm going up to LaCanada to see Doreen Harris, then I'm heading up to Lancaster to see Dean Calico."

"Hell, I'll meet you up there," he said.

I also mentioned that after I left Dean I was heading up to Lake Isabella to see Cortez Hunter.

"Maybe you can ask Cortez to come to Lancaster," he said, "then all three of us can get together."

"Great idea, Jim, I'll call you in a day or two as soon as I get things lined up."

Well, I thought, this may have been how the reunions got started. Soares, Stefani, Rodrigues and a few other California boys may have been talking. "Let's go over and see old so-and-so," somebody might have said.

"Good idea," could have been the reply, "I'll go with you."

But that was in the late 1940's. And now there aren't many old so-and-so's to go over and visit anymore.

EIGHT

After I said goodbye to Jim Oxford, I drove back on the freeway toward my hotel in Westwood. It was a warm Sunday in January, and I had nothing to do for the rest of the day except figure out where I'd have dinner that night. It was a pleasant day, too nice to buck the freeway, so I decided to cut over to Ventura Boulevard and then head south from there through Laurel Canyon to my hotel.

I left my rental car with the hotel doorman and walked into the lobby. I was staying at the Westwood Marquis, a hotel absurdly beyond my means. I had a weekend rate plus a corporate rate and still I was over my head. I went up to my room and looked over a map of the L.A. area. Monday bright and early I would head up to La Canada in the foothills of the San Gabriel Mountains to visit Ed Harris's widow.

I lay down on the couch in my elegant suite and read *The Los Angeles Times*. I was lonely and craved companionship. I couldn't think of anyone I knew well enough to call. My son and his family had moved back to Chicago about a year before, and my only friends dated back to the war years, a few distant cousins on my father's side but now only phantom faces. And then there was Anita. I picked up the telephone book and began searching through the D's, for Durchin, her maiden name. If she had been alive, she would be in her 70's. If she had been married, there would be no way to locate her unless there was another listing for her family name, a relative perhaps by the same name who might know her whereabouts. The other possibility was that she had been divorced and was using her maiden name. But there were no listings whatsoever. Not a clue. She was out of my life as suddenly as she had entered it. But even if I had seen her name staring up at me on the page, I'm not sure if I would have had the courage to call her. After fifty years, how could she possibly remember me. And how could I have dealt with the "who?" — that deadliest of all words — which most surely would have been her response. But I would have risked it. She meant so much to me during the war.

Doreen Harris lives in a modest single story home on a quiet street just off Foothill Boulevard in La Canada. Two large orange trees stand like sentries on the lawn, one on either side of the sidewalk leading up to her front door. She is a pleasant, petite woman, considerably younger than her late husband. I had first met her at a reunion in the early 1980's and then again at our fiftieth in Riverside in 1993, two years after Ed died.

I remember her at the earlier gathering as a somewhat disgruntled participant, seemingly unhappy over having sacrificed her husband as well as some of their income toward perpetuating our reunions. It was easy to figure out why she felt that way, for Ed was a man with a single bee in his bonnet, a mania for keeping the reunions going and for building the men of the 124th into a family, his family, one that would meet every year, no matter what. She sat across from me in her living room, a picture of her daughter and grandchild on an end table next to her chair. I asked her to tell me a little about Ed and how he got so deeply involved in our annual meetings.

"Well, Ed was working for Sparklettes," she said, "and one day a postcard came to the house. That's what started it all."

"The reunions, you mean?"

"Yes, the card was from Ed Soares and Tony Rodrigues. They wanted Ed to come to a reunion, I forget where, somewhere in California. It was mostly boys from California. They had all been in the same battery with Ed."

"D battery?"

"Yes. Well, from then on he was hooked. After that, Ed's whole life was lived for reunions."

She asked if I would like coffee. I nodded, and she excused herself.

When she left the room I strolled into a small den off the living room. There were photos of Ed everywhere — Ed as one of the players on Joe E. Brown's semi-pro baseball team; Ed as an umpire in the Bay State League; Ed as an umpire in the Western International League. All told, he umpired for 52 years, working in addition in the Evangeline League, the Sally League, the Sunset League, and the Three-I League.

"Quite a gallery," I said, as she returned with the coffee.

"Oh, yes," she said. "Ed loved baseball. Umpiring was his life after the army. When he was with the Bay State League, he began looking up his army buddies. He was always looking for his buddies. It never ended. The search was an obsession."

"Ed had almost no knowledge of his background, and what little he did know he never talked about... he obviously had need for a family. The 124th were his boys, his family."

Ed was 85 when he died. He was the oldest man in the battalion. His background was Irish and Polish. His mother died when he was five. He was raised as a foster child.

"Ed had almost no knowledge of his background, and what little he did know he never talked about," she said.

"I didn't know that," I said. "Do you think that had something to do with his searching for buddies, the siblings he never had?"

"He always talked about not having his own family," she said, "so I suppose it did. He obviously had a need for a family. The 124th were his boys, his family. He was especially close to Paul Heiser. You know Paul, don't you?"

"Of course," I said. "Paul's a nice guy."

"Yes he is. Well, Paul was sort of adopted by Ed. He took Paul under his wing and treated him like a son."

She took a quick sip of coffee.

"Please go on, Doreen. Tell me more about Ed."

"Well, all the men meant so much to Ed that we couldn't go on vacation without visiting someone in the outfit. The only places we went were places where someone lived. Ed would go through telephone directories and city directories to locate someone, and then leave me sitting in a motel room without telling me where he was going or when he was coming back."

There was no mistaking her displeasure as she recounted how Ed's search for his buddies had dominated their lives.

Ed was a short, heavy set man with a full head of hair, bushy eyebrows, and a voice like Andy Devine. He wrote to me frequently, especially during the weeks preceeding a reunion. The letters were all the same, desperate pleas to help him round up the troops and get them to attend. He hounded and he pleaded and he spent a slew of his own money on postage and travel. When some of the men explained that they didn't have the money to make the trip, Ed would pay their travel expenses. He was not particularly well-off, but he gave his money and time freely. His commitment to the 124th was so strong that he had to do it.

Money, of course, meant very little to him. Much of what he

earned he gave away, and I think that Doreen may have resented this, too. I recall the time when Ed sent me a shearling jacket, the kind the actor Dennis Weaver wore in the TV series, *Lucas McCord*. There was no reason for it other than his remarkable generosity. For example, he gave enormous chunks of time to Peppermint Ridge, a facility for handicapped children in Corona and to the Braille Institute, where he worked with the blind, the latter a rather interesting irony for a man who more than once in his career as an umpire had himself been called blind.

Doreen took another sip of coffee, and I brought the subject around to Paul Heiser.

"Paul doesn't look any older today than he did in the army," I said. "Still the same sweet guy. He and his wife, Faythe, were on our trip to Dover."

"I'd heard that."

"They're a wonderful couple. We all went to a Sunday morning service," I said, "and I remember watching Paul in church. You could hear his voice over everyone's. He sang the hymns like he really enjoyed them."

"That sounds like Paul," she said.

"Ed would have been in heaven on that trip. If he'd been alive when the trip was organized we'd have had more guys show up, that's for sure."

She smiled. But no doubt, beneath the smile, there was the horrifying thought of Ed buying airplane tickets to England for the guys who couldn't afford the trip.

"It's sad in a way that some of the men weren't as generous as Ed was," I said. "I don't mean only in paying for the reunion trips, but in everything — contributing to Peppermint Ridge, to the Braille Institute, the whole thing."

"Bo Smith helped a lot on Peppermint Ridge," she reminded me.

"And Ralph Olsen, too," I said. "Ralph tried to get yearly contributions from the men, but he wasn't the fund-raising type, I guess, and neither am I. In fairness, you really can't expect one man's cause to rub off on the next guy."

"Of course not," she said.

"Ralph and Phyllis are very decent people," I said.

She nodded.

"They drove down to Portland one night to hear me speak," I said.

"Oh? What was that about?"

"It was at the Jewish Community Center there. I gave a talk on early Jewish settlers in the West. Anyway, I had called Ralph to say I'd be out his way, never thinking he'd show up. I couldn't get over it when I saw them in the audience. He lives up in Vancouver, you know."

"What a nice thing for them to do," she said.

I had gotten to know Paul Heiser, Ed's "adopted son," quite well. He's exactly my age but looks a lot younger. He has five children, 12 grandchildren and one great grandchild. All of this is hard to fathom from looking at him. He and Faythe live in Fostoria, Ohio, where he has spent most of his working life as an accountant with the various corporate entities of Electric Auto-Lite Co. He is a graduate of Bowling Green University.

Paul seems to me to be the most well adjusted man in the battalion. One look at him would tell you that you could trust him with your watch, your wife and your bankroll. He is a happy, church-going, upbeat fellow who would appear never to have been in the grip of a dark thought. To Paul, there are no sad memories at reunions, just a lot of fun meeting his old buddies. He makes reunions part of his annual vacation. He is the only one of us who believes the world is a better place today than when we were discharged.

Not surprisingly for an "adopted son," Paul had many things in common with Ed. Ed eschewed sentimentality; so does Paul. Ed was a shaker and mover. When he put his mind to something, he couldn't be stopped. I detect the same quality in Paul. In addition, I never heard either of them complain.

I asked Doreen if I was right, that Ed never complained about anything.

"You're wrong," she said. "He complained frequently, and

sometimes bitterly."

"I'm surprised," I said. "What about?"

"Just one thing," she said, "only one."

"What was that?"

"He thought the world was going to the dogs."

"He has plenty of company there," I said.

I stood up to leave.

"Wait a minute," she said, "I'll walk you to your car."

We walked down the sidewalk toward the street, and I stopped briefly to admire the two orange trees on the lawn.

"By the way, Doreen, given Ed's feeling of family, I guess he took it pretty hard when one of the gang passed away. How much did it affect him? A lot of us are gone, you know."

She smiled.

What a pretty woman, I thought.

"He mourned them, all right," she said, "but they were the only people he did mourn. Just his army buddies, and maybe some dead ballplayers."

NINE

The death of a buddy has been the best kept secret in the battalion. There was never an announcement at a reunion of the men who had died during the previous year, nor was there ever a reference to a death in any of the mailings that were sent out twice a year. I eventually concluded that there was an unwritten, unspoken understanding that Death, as a concept, did not exist in the 124th. It had no place in our battalion even though every year reunion attendance was shrinking. It was the ultimate denial. Ed Harris's persistence in tracking down men was, only by accident, the way I got the news of somebody's death. Let me explain how.

In advance of a reunion, Ed, as I mentioned, would write a flurry of letters to various men, prodding and bullying them to write to others, usually those whose attendance had been poor over the years.

"Write O'Brien and tell him to write to Magliochetti, then write Ed Bandur and have him write Herb Cottier and tell Herb to try to reach Lukasik..." And so the letters went, over and over, until it was nearly time for our gathering. He never let up, and you always felt that if you didn't do exactly as he said you'd be betraying one of the most beloved men in the battalion. Beloved yes, but also irascible.

Ed would never mention someone's death, but he wrote his letters on the back side of the copies of the pages listing the names and addresses of all the men, circling in red those he wanted you to write to along with the cryptic notation, "Write." Frequently I would note that a man's name was a crossed out with the word "deceased" alongside it, and in this way, through Ed's notations to himself, I'd find out who was either dead or untraceable.

As the man who ran the show, it was undoubtedly up to Ed Soares to make such announcements, either by mail or from the podium at our Saturday afternoon business meetings, meetings that were usually devoted to voting on where the next year's event would be held. I remember standing up at a meeting several years ago and announcing that my pal Danny Ciccelli had passed away. Ed had glared at me from the podium and immediately went on to another subject. It was then that I realized that a buddy's passing was not to be noted publicly. And it never had been until our 54th reunion in Scottsdale when the recently deceased men were listed on a sheet of paper.

I remember my resentment in not knowing about the death of Herman Reading, a gunner in A Battery. Herman and I didn't

The author and Herman Reading (figures 6 and 7 from left) in a railroad station in France enroute home.

get along too well during the war, when we were both boys, but later as old men we became close friends. He passed away late in 1992. He was a happy good natured fellow who in later years operated a tavern in Sturtevant, Wisconsin. Herman brought his wife to the reunions as well as his daughter and son-in-law. All of them were heavy smokers and beer drinkers. At reunions, long after most of the men and their wives had retired for the evening, you could find the Reading family closing the bar at the various hotels and motels where we met. Saloons were Herman's business, his avocation, his life. He died much too young. It was too bad. There were so many more bars to close up, so much more life to be enjoyed.

I learned about his death when I checked into the Riverside Hilton for our 50th reunion. I saw Herman's wife in the lobby. She was with her daughter. I approached her.

"Hi, Lois," I said, "where's Herman?"

She stared at me blankly as if she hadn't understood my question.

A small woman with blond hair, she confused me with her silence. I fully expected her to tell me that Herman was up in his room taking a nap. Instead, she hesitated a moment and then told me that Herman had been dead for over a year.

I felt my knees buckling. I thought of this wiry little man with whom I scrapped so many times during the war. Although our squabbles were sometimes bitter, they ended with Herman's laugh and big wide grin and our hands clasped in a firm grip of fellowship while I, glad to know we were still friends, struggled to keep my tears of relief in check. Something went out of me at the thought of a reunion without Herman. He was my friend. Why hadn't I been told? Why was it a secret?

At our 54th reunion, when I saw the names of the deceased written in the hospitality suite, for all to see, it came as a breakthrough. I've tried to sort out the reasons for the silence over the years as well as for the sudden coming clean. I'm puzzled by it. I can only surmise how hard it must have been for Ed Soares and Bo Smith and others of our shakers and movers to acknowledge the loss of a comrade, for by denying a death, it would seem, the battalion remains, figuratively at least, at full strength, ready to do battle again, capable of surviving forever, or until the last man has gone.

"Any man's death diminishes me," wrote John Donne — and hence, in large measure, that man's death diminishes the battalion as a whole.

TEN

I called Cortez Hunter from Lancaster, California, a desert town of some 40,000, located near Edwards Air Force Base. I wanted to find out if he'd be free that day for a late lunch. He lived in Lake Isabella, a small mountain community about forty miles from Bakersfield.

"Where are you now?" he asked.

"In Lancaster. I just had breakfast with Dean Calico."

It was good hearing his voice. He was a likeable fellow from A Battery. Although we were never close during the war, we always got along splendidly in the years following. Since then we established a fairly close bond.

"How is old Dean?" he asked.

"Seems fine," I said. "You know he had cancer, but I think he's got it licked. I hope so."

"Yeah, I heard about it. Were you thinking of driving up here?" he asked.

"Sure, if you've got the time."

He laughed.

"I got plenty of that," he said.

"I could come up to Lake Isabella or meet you in Bakersfield, either way."

He paused for a moment. Lake Isabella was located somewhat farther away, a remote community northeast of Bakersfield, and I was hoping he'd suggest Bakersfield. I wanted to get back to L.A. before dark, Lord knows why. Part of my overwhelming wish

115

to be back to the bright lights of Hollywood, I guess. There it was, the persistent theme of my life: the allure of the romantic past overpowering the sleaze of the present.

"Naw, I've got another idea. I think I'll drive down to Mojave and meet you there," he said. "It'll give me something to do."

I'd have driven almost anywhere to meet him, but I have to admit I was a bit relieved. Mojave was just 40 miles north of Lancaster, and it would save me about two hours of driving.

"Are you sure you don't mind?"

"Hell, no," he said. "When you get into town, there's a Scottish Inn right on the main drag. I'll meet you in their parking lot."

"What's a good time for you?"

"Let's see. How about one o'clock. I need a few hours to get out of my overalls and get down there."

"Couldn't be better."

"I operated a motel for about three years. It was my inlaws' motel and I took it over after they died. Those were the worst three years of my life, a hell of a lot worse than the army. The army was nothing compared to that."

"We'll have lunch in Mojave," he said.

After I hung up, I checked out of my motel and decided to drive around Lancaster. I had plenty of time. Lancaster was not a very appealing town. There were lines forming in front of state unemployment offices, men and women both looking for day labor, and I thought of the time, two years after I got out of the army, when I hitchhiked to California with Dan Marder, a friend of mine from college. Neither of us had money and we did various odd jobs along the way, working our way up the coast from L.A. We iced lettuce in Salinas and picked fruit in Watsonville and Santa Cruz and saved what little money we earned for nights drinking beer in bars with names like "New Bataan Cafe." I thought of all the small Filipino men who worked in the fields all day, then came home and got cleaned up and put on their light beige gabardine suits and pointed Stacy Adams shoes, and went looking for fair skinned blondes. At night, they sat around the cafes listening to the music and feeling sad as some gorgeous Asian singer sang the popular songs of the day, often parroting the English lyrics in a heart-sick phonetic wail. I thought about these things as I drove north on Route 29 toward Mojave. I was a long way from the coast and the Watsonville of the 40's, but what was the difference. California is California, a land of starlets and fruitpickers and millions of wayward souls. I loved it then, and I love it today, and I had a strong sense of well-being driving through the high desert on my way to see Cortez. I could have been anywhere in the state — Hollywood, Riverside, Barstow or Watsonville and I would still feel the magic.

The scenes of fifty years ago haunt me — the beautiful Asian girl in a satin gown singing "I Understand" in a dive in Watsonville, her body movements out of sinc with the lyrics, her utter lack of comprehension of the words to the song all too obvious. Yet what did it matter — she knew the music and she knew what sadness was all about, and as the words poured forth, I sat dreaming of an exquisite night in the arms of this sultry, dark-skinned beauty, while at the same time the Filipino men most likely were dreaming of holding onto the arm of a tall blonde chick and parading her like a trophy down the streets of Watsonville, their spotless beige gabardine suits darted at the waist, the crease in their trousers razor-sharp. She sang:

> I understand,
> And darling you are not to blame
> If when we kiss it's not the same,
> I understand.

Could I, I wondered, have been any more out of touch with the 1990's than she was with the words to her song? Here I was in the California that I loved in the 1940's imagining, beyond its modern day repugnance, that nothing had changed, that it was still a civilized and attractive place where blonde beauties could be catapulted to stardom directly from the stool of a soda fountain.

I had breakfast with Dean Calico in Lancaster an hour or so earlier. We met in a restaurant adjoining my motel. He had brought his wife, Wilda. They were waiting for me in a booth when I arrived. They were stiff and apprehensive, wondering what my visit was about. We were friendly in the army but not very close.

I had seen him at a reunion in Las Vegas some ten years earlier, and he hadn't changed much since then. In fact, he still looked pretty much like he did in the army, except that he had become much heavier. Wilda's presence surprised me. I hadn't figured on any of the men bringing their wives, and it was a little bit inhibiting. I judged that the two of them were inseparable. Dean has retired. Wilda is a cosmetician.

Dean is almost exactly my age. He had been living in Lancaster since 1935 and since 1956 had worked at various jobs at Edwards Air Force Base. He is polite and agreeable, but not one of our more ardent reunion goers — in fact he had attended only four since 1953. I was searching for some understanding as to why that was or how he differed in his overall attitudes from those men who were like myself. The only discernible difference I could come up with was his reserve; he appeared to be far less emotional, more dispassionate, than the men who were hooked on reunions. He was just as matter-of-fact about his having cancer. He was not shy about it, and seemed thankful about being on the mend. He did not appear involved with his illness, as I would have been. He had worked in fuel on experimental aircraft at Edwards, and his attitude toward confronting his illness must have had the same dispassionate quality as tackling a leaky fuel compartment on a fighter-bomber.

He told me he had disliked some of the guys during the war but no longer felt that way. The individual friendships that started years ago have continued to be strong, he said, but he has no feeling for the battalion as a whole. He spoke fondly of his long-standing friendship with Ed Erickson, another gunner in A battery, but mentioned that Erickson had died, something I hadn't been aware of. I have a snapshot of Dean and Ed Erickson, taken as they waited their turns in a barbershop at Konigsee. Their friendship had been close for half a century.

Thinking about that snapshot awakened memories of Konigsee, a startlingly beautiful mountain lake in the Alps where the battalion was sent for R&R.. The mountain called Watzmann was just to the north and always in view; to our south was the Eagle's Nest, Hitler's retreat at Berchtesgaden. It was early summer and the war in Europe had ended. The lake was restful and serene. The entire setting — the mountains, the lake in the foreground, the feeling of total seclusion, were strikingly different from the war we had left to the north. I was so taken by the beauty of the place that I longed to share it with someone who meant something to me. But there was no one. By this time, Anita and I had stopped corresponding. The mere exchanging of letters couldn't sustain a relationship grounded in but two evenings together and no sex. One or two quick embraces outside the Tail O'the Cock don't count.

The battalion was billeted in two hotels, both overlooking the lake, the Hotel Konigsee and the Hotel Schiffmeister. I sent a color brochure of the latter to the only person who would be interested — my mother. I drew an arrow pointing to one of the rooms in the photograph, noting untruthfully that it was the very same room in which I was staying. Many years later, after my mother died, I found the brochure in a strongbox in which she kept her valuable papers. She had kept it all those years. I don't believe any of her possessions affected me as much as seeing that old dog-eared brochure with all its poignant memories.

Dean and Wilda are a couple in every sense of the word—a joined at the hip, feeling-sharing, mutually reliant couple. This is readily apparent, for instance, in their dislike (sometimes bordering on hatred) for another couple, President Clinton and his wife. Not on one issue but on all of them. It is the Clinton's liberal point of view versus the Calico's staunch conservatism. However they aren't unusual in that regard. There aren't many liberals in the 124th.

I arrived at the Scottish Inn parking lot in Mojave promptly at one. Cortez arrived a few minutes later. He had brought along his younger brother, another Dean, for company. They both live in the town of Lake Isabella.

We parked our cars and walked next door to a restaurant and sat down in a booth. In order to put me at ease, Cortez, in good humor, mentioned that he had Parkinson's disease although he needn't have: it was quite evident from his tremors. Apart from that, he looked quite healthy. He was a jovial man with a ruddy face who had grown quite heavy over the years.

The three of us had a good lunch, and while we were eating I explained what I was up to and how important I thought it was to create a record of some sort about our battalion and our passion for getting together every year.

"My kids and grandkids might be the only ones who'd be interested," I said, "and I'm not even sure about them."

"How many you got?" he asked.

"Three kids, five grandkids," I said. "How about you?"

"Almost the same," he said. "Two kids, five grandkids."

He had been a corporal in A battery during the war, and had spent most of his post-war years as a worker in the institutional fence business. When I mentioned that I had visited Doreen Harris, a few days earlier, he said that Ed Harris had once tracked him down on a job site, just as he had so many others. At the time, he explained, Ed had been in Bakersfield umpiring.

Cortez is typical of so many other men of the 124th. He passionately hated the army but now is an inveterate reunion goer.

"There are times," he said, "when you look back and think you had a good time."

I nodded.

"I guess that's because when you get old you forget the bad things and remember the good times," I said.

"Yeah, but you couldn't have told me that at the time. I sure didn't want to see anyone in our outfit again when I got out. I remember walking down Main Street in LA. just after I was discharged. I started throwing away my army clothing one piece at a time, just walking along throwing things away."

He told me he had retired at 59, some eleven years earlier.

"Had you been in fence construction all your working years?" I asked.

"Most but not all of them. I operated a motel for about three years," he said. "It was my in-laws' motel and I took it over after they died. Those were the worst three years of my life, a hell of a lot worse than the army. The army was nothing compared to that."

"What are you up to now?" I asked.

"Nothin' much. I spend most of my time fishing in Lake Isabella."

"Well, you must like it living up there but what else do you do when you're not fishing?"

"Not much. Me and Dean hang out at El Rancho No-Got drinking beer."

"El Rancho what?" I asked.

"No-Got."

I laughed.

"I guess that means everyone is welcome who hasn't got a pot to piss in," I said.

"That's right."

"Well, save me a stool," I said.

Cortez paid the check and three of us walked out to his car.

"I want to show you something," he said.

He opened his trunk and pulled out a cardboard box. It was crammed with old photos and mementos from the war. I was impressed with the way he had hung onto things.

"I think you're like me," I said. "Can't let go of things."

"Well, no," he replied. "I keep this stuff up in the attic because my kids used to go through it, but I don't pay it any mind anymore. When you called, I threw it in the truck in case you wanted to look it over."

"I appreciate it," I said.

We went through the photographs, one at a time, two old guys, backs to the highway, sadly lost in thoughts of the past. Instead of soft music playing in the background, there was only the sound of eighteen-wheelers roaring up and down route 29. As we stood there, we either laughed or shook our heads despairingly, depending on whether the man in the photograph was alive or dead. And if we didn't know, one of us would say: I wonder what happened to old so-and-so. Sometimes we would grope for a man's name, usually some of Mexican guys like Villareal or Contreras or Matamoros.

I told him I'd missed him at our 50th reunion in Riverside.

"I don't know what the hell happened, I just couldn't get down there."

"I missed seeing you and I got a little worried."

"Naw, I wasn't sick or anything," he said. "Something came up, I can't remember what."

"I don't think I'd ever been to a reunion that I didn't see you and your wife," I said.

"I think I've made most of them."

"You're coming to Phoenix, aren't you?" I said, referring to our next roundup.

"Oh, sure. I'd come even if there were only two of us left."

He showed me a rolled up photo, about three feet wide, taken early in 1943. It was of B Battery at Camp Callan where we took our basic training. One by one I looked at all the faces, eighteen and nineteen year olds along with a sprinkling of older guys, a look of hard-eyed determination on each face. All but the officers and non-coms were no more than three months away from their mammys' kitchens, and some of them still piss'n-abed, as they say.

He asked me if I'd like to take the photograph with me.

I nodded.

I scanned the faces in the picture. Mine was not among them. I didn't get it. Most of the B Battery guys from Callan went on to become members of A Battery at Camp Haan when the 124th was formed. Where was I anyway? Here was a photograph of all my comrades and I wasn't among them.

"As I recall," Cortez explained, "you and a few other guys were assigned to D Battery."

"Glad you told me," I said. "My memory is gone."

I held up the rolled up photograph and tapped it lovingly.

"I'll get this back to you soon," I said.

"No hurry."

We shook hands.

"See you in Phoenix," I said.

I said goodbye to Dean, got back in my car and headed down Route 29 toward L.A.

Was it really so long ago that I left the one-room apartment in Chicago that I shared with my mother and went off to Camp Grant, Illinois, the induction center. Not that long ago, surely, to account for my nearly total absence of recollection of those first three months in the army. Worst of all was not even remembering what battery I was assigned to. My memory of that short block of time can't be jogged, not even if I were to grab it with both hands and choke it. I am able to reconstruct nearly every turn in the road since I was three, but trying to recall those early days of basic training is like coming to a washed out bridge. Nowhere to go but to detour around it. Had basic training been so routine, so monotonously regimented that only the most percipient individual would be able to retain any of the humdrum elements of it? Oh, the mysteries of the human mind.

ELEVEN

Alvin "Huey" Long lives in a Planned Unit Development in Chandler, Arizona, a sprawling community about forty miles southeast of Phoenix. Coming off Interstate 10 into Chandler, I was struck by just how new the city appeared to be. Recently built one-story southwestern style homes were lined up like rows of planted beans, seemingly having sprung up out of the desert with their TV antennas in place.

As close as I was to the men of the 124th, I still had only a fuzzy image of what Huey looked like. He was a gunner in D Battery and a reunion regular but we never had a chance to get acquainted. There had been no chance during the war since each of the battalion's five batteries were usually positioned a few miles apart from one another. It was somewhat the same story at our reunions. The men from each battery socialized mainly amongst themselves; my own close friends were members of A battery. I did develop friendships with some of the men from other batteries, but up until the time I visited Huey he had not been one of them.

This raises the question of why I chose to talk with Huey instead of with some of the men I knew better. The truth is that I wanted to visit Phoenix, a city that holds me in its grip just as southern California does. Huey, as it happened, was the only guy in the battalion who lived in the general area.

The Phoenix of today is very different from the Phoenix of my early teens. The city at that time had a population of 65,000 compared with nearly two-million today, but even though there are only a few places left standing that look familiar to me, I still go back to visit every few years. I can't help myself. On every visit I drive past my old apartment building at Central and McDowell. The building's sub-structure hasn't changed but with each new pilgrimage I notice a new face on the building. It's had more face lifts than an aging movie star. But I look right past these cosmetic changes and directly into our one-room apartment where I can still hear Rex Alderdice and my mother talking while I feigned sleep on the in-a-door bed.

These days, newcomers to Phoenix as well as the tourists by-pass the city in favor of the newer, more fashionable Scottsdale and Paradise Valley. I'm glad they do. It leaves the city proper to me, to cruise around as I wish down the streets I once knew. But I remember nothing that now is there. There was a time, however, when I walked to school along those streets or rode my bike on them and delivered the *Arizona Republic* on them. Now even the Arizona State Hospital, at 24th and Van Buren, a terrifying gray stone edifice surrounded by a barbed-wire fence, is no longer standing, having been replaced by modern one-story dormitories. When I was young I was sure that the murderess, Winnie Ruth Judd, was watching my every move from her cell facing Van Buren street. Oh, Phoenix, one of my many lost loves!

Once I arrived in Chandler, it took me a while to find out where Huey lived. I made several wrong turns, and finally pulled into an older development of modest flat roofed homes off Alma School Road. From the outside, all the units looked alike — all with light tan stucco exteriors, and each with a carport. I located his unit and rang the bell. A moment later, the door opened and there was Huey, a big, good natured fellow with a wide smile. He greeted me with a hand shake and invited me in.

"Did you have any trouble getting here?"

"None whatsoever. I only had to stop twice to get directions. Not bad for a guy who went to scouting and patrolling school," I said.

He laughed.

I looked around the house. It was comfortably furnished with overstuffed furniture, and displayed numerous touches that only a woman could have had a hand in. It was late in the afternoon. His wife was nowhere to be seen and I figured that she had gone out to run errands or something of the sort in order to give Huey and me some time together.

At first I didn't think he understood exactly what I was up to because he began reviewing his army experiences without being asked. It sounded like he had already rehearsed what he was going to talk about. He told me that his army career had been a disappointment. He never progressed very far, he said, in spite of some early success in basic training. He had made corporal shortly before we went overseas and had never gone beyond that rank. I assured him that I hadn't done very well either, and I think it may have surprised him that pfc was the highest rank I had attained.

He told me he was born and raised in Forgan, Oklahoma, in the Oklahoma panhandle. Right after Pearl Harbor, he wanted to enlist but his older sister persuaded him to hold off until he was nineteen. Finally drafted in March of 1943, he was then inducted at Fort Sill, Oklahoma, and from there was shipped to Camp Callan. He explained that he had gotten off to a fast start at Callan and immediately was made a gun commander in addition to being appointed barracks orderly.

"You must have made one hell of an impression right off the bat," I said.

"Naw, it wasn't that," he replied, "it's just that I had some work experience under my belt. They saw that on my records."

"What kind of job did you have?" I asked.

"Well, it wasn't exactly a job. I was going to high school and was in the National Youth Administration. I got paid for doing odd jobs around the school. Thirty-five cents an hour."

"Not bad for the times," I said.

"It came in damn handy, I'll tell you."

"Besides that, National Youth Administration must have impressed hell out of the officers," I said. "It sounds important."

"Probably so," he said, "but it didn't do me any good once I got to Camp Haan. I wasn't a gun commander any longer, just a member of a gun crew in D Battery. Some of the time I alternated as a carpenter's helper."

I had to use the john during our talk, and he led me down a short hallway toward the bathroom. It was tidy and clean. The towels were neatly folded and bric-a-brac and framed mottos covered the walls. For a 280 pounder, he seemed to adjust nicely into a small house dotted everywhere with feminine touches. He was light on his feet, defying the bull-in-the-china-shop cliche.

Before I returned to the living room, I glanced at my watch. It was getting on toward five and I expected his wife to be returning at any time to fix dinner. I had other matters to cover with him but I didn't want to overstay my welcome and interfere with their evening meal. My instincts told me that he and his wife would probably have their supper at an early hour.

When I returned to the living room, I asked him to let me know when he wanted to me leave.

"I don't want to get in your wife's hair when she gets home," I said.

"You won't," he said. "Stay as long as you like. My wife died in 1992."

"I'm sorry to hear that," I said.

I paused and looked around the room. He evidently hadn't touched a thing since his wife died. It was as if she had walked out of the house one day to go shopping and had never come back. Everything seemed to be just as she had left it.

He talked about his wife rather matter of factly as though he were reporting a lousy bowling score. With Huey, life goes on, I thought. I envied the attitude.

He then told me that he had been married twice and widowed twice. He lost his first wife in 1976 after a 28 year marriage, his second wife after 17 years. There were children from both marriages. He explained that he remained close to all of the children.

"Don't you get lonely, living by yourself?" I asked. "I know I sure as hell would."

He waved off my concern.

"I keep pretty busy," he said. "I go down to the Elks Club a lot and I get together with some friends pretty often."

Our fifty-first reunion was to be held in Phoenix in October, 1994. Huey was one of the chairmen, sharing some of the responsibility for staging the event with Ed Soares's daughter, Tina.

Huey has missed only a few reunions since 1953.

"Some of my friends from around here can hardly believe we get together every year. They never heard the likes of it," he said.

He told me that the reunions weren't just a lark.

"They're very important. I look forward to them about three months in advance," he said.

"We've lost quite a few men in the past few years," I said.

"I know," he said. "I get busted up every time I hear a buddy died."

I asked him if he thought we'd continue having our get-togethers even though a lot of the guys are dead or too sick to travel.

"The reunions won't ever die," he replied. "If five guys were left we'd still meet."

He talked about his late wife rather matter-of-factly as though he were reporting a lousy bowling score. With Huey, life goes on. I envied the attitude.

129

"What about you and just one other survivor. Would you meet every year then?"

"Hell, yes," he replied.

"I don't know about you, Huey, but I wonder if we'd have much left to say to each other if we met much longer."

"We don't have to talk," he said.

"I know what you mean," I said.

It was getting late. I wanted to get back to Phoenix for dinner.

"I've got one more question for you," I said, as I stood up to leave

"Fire away. Ask as many as you want."

"I was just wondering what you thought about the world today compared with when we were discharged."

He thought for a moment.

"Well, financially I'm better off." he replied. "I've got my social security and a pension from my old company. But other than that it was a better world then."

"Yes it was," I said, "it sure was."

TWELVE

A couple of years after I left the army I realized how ignorant I was about my wartime service overseas. I knew what countries I was in, of course, but I had no idea exactly where I was within those countries. I knew, for example, that for awhile I was in or around Leeds, which was in the north of England, and that later on I was in Kent along the Dover coast. But where exactly were they? I had no frame of reference for either place. For one thing I hadn't studied geography in high school and had only a fragment of the subject in grammar school. Furthermore, the army wasn't passing out travel folders or road maps, much less maps of any kind, to lowly enlisted men like myself. It was the same story on the continent. I knew I was in France and Belgium and Holland and Germany, but my location in these countries was no more precise than knowing that I was in the north or south, the east or west.

My lack of awareness of geography was one thing, but being unaware of the fighting taking place around me was even more shocking. I had no sense of the actual progress of the war, no knowledge of the advances and retreats of our armies and theirs at given times, and not even a glimmer of how the German army was structured, much less of how ours was.

I have a friend named Ed Singleton who was a medic in Headquarters Battery. I see him on occasion, and we enjoy reminiscing about the war. But he will frequently mention incidents that I can't recall, and he in turn will go blank when I bring up other matters. It is clear that we each had remembered different things, had forgotten other things, even though we were in the same battalion and never too far from each other. He had recalled the war, it seemed, just as I had, as a series of disconnected events, like pieces from a jigsaw puzzle that never match up. We had been kids in boots, somewhere on foreign soil, uneducated, inexperienced, and lacking in any global comprehension, living in a world composed of only the ground we stood on, either snow-covered and frozen, or else muddy and rut-filled from the big cats that pulled our 90-millimeter guns. In the eight months that we were in actual combat, it was the only ground that I can remember.

I recall dining in a restaurant with my wife a few years ago when an acquaintance of ours, a lawyer a number of years younger than I, walked in. We invited him to join us. As we talked, the subject of World War II came up. He fancied himself an authority on the European theater. He talked to me about the various engagements and wanted to know which division my outfit was assigned to and whether we had participated in such-and-such a battle. When he asked where I was during the Battle of the Bulge, I could only blurt out, "somewhere near Aachen, I think." As I later recalled, we were trapped near Gulpen, Holland. I didn't know that at the time, however. But no matter. I was becoming increasing ill at ease. Here was a man who only read about the war while I, who had been in the thick of things, wasn't even able to carry on a conversation with him. I was annoyed with him but more so with myself for my ignorance. After we said goodbye I felt sure I had left him with the conviction that I had never spent a day in service.

Not only didn't I know where I was half the time, I was also in the dark about the progress of the war. I had an uncle named Harry Davidson who in his patronizing way kept me abreast of the action. Harry lived in Des Moines, Iowa, all his life, leaving the city only infrequently. He was a wildly emotional man whose reaction to people was as changing and turbulent as a hurricane, ranging from rhapsodic affection on one hand to fierce hatred on the other. He hated Adolph Hitler so violently it defies description, and it was Uncle Harry's one consistent emotion.

After I left for the army, he began corresponding with me, each letter conveying his hatred for Hitler along with a plea to go out and kill those "Nazi rat bastards," as if I were a child playing war with a tin helmet and toy pistol. But then he would go on to write me about what the real men in the real army were accomplishing. Here he would give me a status report on the war. His material came directly from the radio where night after night he would listen to reports of Edward R. Murrow and Gabriel Heatter.

His letters to me while I was in combat were written in a manner suggesting that I was off in Fort Des Moines, a few miles down the road, at the WAC training camp, and like himself was merely an interested third party. No matter how much his letters annoyed me they did provide a summary of the fighting. Apart from some back issues of *Yank* and *Star and Stripes* and fragments from the armed forces radio network, it was the only source I had.

Harry has been dead for many years but I still retain an image of Willie and Joe, Bill Mauldin's cartoon characters, whenever I think about him, and of one cartoon in particular. I'm not sure whether the cartoon ever existed or if I had made it up. The cartoon I visualize shows Willie and Joe, grimy and unshaven, huddled together in a foxhole, mortar shells exploding around them and small arms fire whizzing overhead. They're reading a letter. "Uncle Harry says we've got the Krauts on the run," says one character to the other.

THIRTEEN

My pal Charlie Murchison and I were convinced we had a big career in show business ahead of us if and when we got out of the army. Charlie was an outstanding piano player. He came to the recreation hall at Camp Haan in the evenings after chow and I followed him there. I leaned on the piano and listened as he played songs of the late 1930's and early forties. One was David Rose's "Holiday for Strings." It was a beautiful composition, which we both liked, but because it had no lyrics at the time we decided that it was our personal responsibity to furnish the words, some lyrics we could sing besides da-da-da-da. It was our first collaborative effort, and the lyrics we wrote went something like this:

> While I'm playing
> Something's saying
> Here inside me
> Let it guide me
> To a symphony in strings
> The melody is haunting me
> Its magic theme is taunting me,
> I can't escape it though I try to.

It wasn't the easiest composition to put words to, and we either abandoned the project or I have mercifully forgotten the rest of it. In any event, we didn't try to contact David Rose. Many years later, I heard the song played on the radio with someone doing a vocal, and I thought at the time that the words weren't much better than ours.

As things turned out, Charlie and I did enjoy careers in show-biz, mine of a more marginal nature than his. After college, I went to work as a reporter for *Variety*, a theatrical paper, reviewing night clubs and vaudeville, while Charlie began playing piano in cocktail lounges in communities east of L.A., places like Claremont, Covina, and El Monte, or wherever he could get a booking. He spent most of his career playing piano, having studied music at the L.A. Conservatory. Along the way, he worked in the real estate business, had a stint at a savings and loan in Palos Verde and oper-ated his own restaurant in Lomita, California. In later years he was employed in the marketing department at Bridgestone Tires.

The center of culture in the battalion still lies in Charlie's tal-ented fingers. His piano playing during the war and after is a time-less symbol of the 124th, as important to us as our battalion crest. He has attended a number of reunions, and it's unthinkable for Charlie not to be called upon to play the piano. He knows that he is our connection to the war years. Today as we gather around the piano when he plays, we think of the times when we did the same thing a half-century ago, at Camp Haan, Camp Livingston, Camp Edwards and Camp Myles Standish, even on a horribly out-of-tune piano at a bombed out church in Holland during the Battle of the Bulge. Then, as we listened, we thought about home and the joy of someday returning to civilian life. But now the tables are turned. Nowadays, when Charlie plays, we think about the good old days in the army.

Charlie hasn't changed much over the years. He was the tallest man in the battalion then, and the skinniest, and he still is today. There was no one who had more hair than Charlie, either. It was piled on top of his head like a clump of tumbleweed, and most of it is still there, grayer of course but basically still intact.

Charlie got married within a year after his army discharge, but the marriage didn't last. Shortly after his divorce he married a gal singer, but that didn't last, either. His third try in 1973 to Nita, a fine woman and talented singer from Talequah, Oklahoma, has been one of Charlie's more permanent ventures. They have between them 21 grandchildren, 16 from Charlie's previous marriages, five from Nita's It's hard to imagine Charlie living outside the L.A. area, away from the smoke-filled bars and night clubs where he once earned his living. But for over 20 years he has lived with Nita in Talequah, her home town, on a small acreage on the outskirts of town. His delight in showbiz, however, has not diminished. He eagerly volunteers in Talequah as an accompanist for local theatrical productions. In addition, he was instrumental in forming a local musical group that he calls the "Jazz Lab."

Not long after moving to Talequah he was diagnosed with leukemia. The disease is in remission, and when I visited him in 1994 he was making good progress, but still looked unusually thin. Nevertheless, his good humor is still there, leukemia or not.

During the summer of 1945, shortly after VE Day, the 124th was shipped south to Bavaria, ostensibly to serve as part of the occupation forces. In truth, however, our duties, as far as I could tell, were so loosely defined as to be non-existent. Our real assignment was to hang loose and await deployment to the South Pacific should we be needed. We yearned to go home. We'd had enough war, and the prospect of continuing on in a bleak hell-hole like the South Pacific was a morale-killer.

But without any real duties we had time on our hands. I'm not sure how it got started, but somehow Charlie and I along with a few other men decided to put on a show, just like Mickey Rooney in *Babes in Arms*. It was a way for Charlie and me to keep our hands in showbiz and at the same time gain a little more experience.

I don't discount the possibility that we were influenced by a USO troupe that entertained us at about the same time in an open field in Regensburg, Bavaria, not far from the Czech border. There, seated on the grass, were more G.I.'s and officers than I had ever seen gathered in one place. There were the usual assortment of dancers, together with a band. The show was headlined by comedian Jan Murray, with Mr. Ballantine, the comic magician, also on the bill. I doubt if I'll ever again see a happier or more appreciative audience.

As I recall, there was a strong interest in the entertainment business in the outfit as a whole. I can't say whether the same interest existed in other outfits as well or whether we were unusual. I do remember the heated discussions that took place on several occasions between some of the Italian boys from San Francisco's North Beach area. Sometimes I was included in the arguments, which centered exclusively on popular crooners and their relative merits. I was a strong backer of a Mexican kid named Andy Russell, just to show my independence. The other men, Sangervasi, Duranto, Stefani and Sarubi, among others, went on ad nauseum about Frank Sinatra, Johnny Desmond, Russ Columbo, Perry Como, and the new kid from New York, Vito Farranola, an overnight sensation who had the bobby soxers rioting at the Paramount theater. Later he would straighten his hair and fix his nose and become Vic Damone. Others like Dick Haymes, the Eberle brothers, Bing Crosby and Buddy Clark were acknowledged to be good but no one went to bat for them because they weren't *paisans.*

In the course of putting on our show we demonstrated just how enterprising and ingenious we could be. Musical instruments somehow were appropriated from Czechoslovakia. Charlie with someone else's help managed to secure stock musical arrangements. The call went out for musicians and actors. This was big time stuff. Charlie took over the musical duties, and being a clerk in Headquarters Battery, at the time, he had some communications clout and put out a call for anyone who could play an instrument. I was astounded when a dozen or so musicians turned up from among our scruffy lot of soldiers. Among them were Ray Kreizinger on trombone, Charlie Blackwell on sax, and Charlie Murchison , of course, on piano. Charlie began rehearsing the men, slowly whipping them into shape. It wasn't easy. They had been without practice since their high school marching band days. But after a while they were able to do a creditable job with tunes like "Dream" and "I Should Care" and a few other popular numbers of the time.

So far we had only a band-based show, and it was obvious that we needed other types of entertainment to go with it. The backbone of every musical revue, of course, is a chorus line, so our next step was to find some hairy looking animals from among the troops and dress them up like women (drag was a word that hadn't yet come into play at the time). The chorus line consisted of six men, Earl White and Hank Stefani being two of the group that I can remember. We didn't try to make them look "cute," for that would have been impossible. Our notion was to have them look like exactly what they were — obnoxious animals dressed up in women's dresses.

My job was to write the skits and tie the entire show together. No one was qualified to do it, least of all myself, but things, I've been told, always work out for the best. My point is that had I not fucked off in high school — just as I had in the army — the show might never have been written. During my four years in high school, I had attended four schools, each in a different city. My education had no continuity, and, with a few exceptions, I had made no real friends at any of the schools. Furthermore, there were no teachers who got to know me well enough to take any interest in a dispirited transient like me. If anything else is to blame for all my educational missteps, it would have to be the lure of the bright lights and excitement of Chicago, all of which were new to me. It was too much competition for Senn High School. Instead of attending classes, I would cut school and attend the matinees at the State Lake, Oriental and Chicago theaters, all vaudeville houses. I saw most of the headliners of the day, including two touring companies, Olsen & Johnson's "Helzapoppin" and Benny Meroff's "Funzapoppin," the latter a blatant knock-off of the first.

Most of the skits in our show came directly from these two shows. It was not a case of good comedy writing on my part but rather grand theft coupled with a good memory. I should have been crowned "The Thief of Badgags," as Milton Berle once was. I still remember some of our skits.

The show opens. The band is playing "Dream," its signature number. One of the men comes down the aisle with a broom and dust pan, pretending to sweep up. "Hey, what's all the commotion," says the master of ceremonies.

"No come on ocean," comes the reply, "come on streetcar right outside." (Rim-shot.)

Man slowly walks across the stage carrying a glass of water. He stares blankly down at the glass. He repeats the process over and over, throughout the show. Each time he passes by with his glass of water, the m.c. throws him a bewildered look, but says nothing. Finally, in total exasperation the m.c. says. "Why in hell are you walking back and forth with that glass of water?"

Without glancing up or breaking stride, the man replies, as if in a trance, "My house in on fire." (Rim-shot.)

Man dressed as swami enters from stage left. "Would you like your palm read," he says to the m.c. The m.c. nods and extends his hand, palm up. Swami reaches into the bucket he carries and removes a paint brush, then slaps the m.c.'s palm with red paint. (Rim-shot.)

Man dressed as gal enters stage right. She has enormous

He walked over to the piano, looked down at the keyboard, and threw me a glance. There was a twinkle in his eye. He played three numbers for me: "Holiday for Strings," "I Should Care," and "Dream." By the time he had finished I had tears in my eyes.

breasts and flounces across the stage like a slut, tossing the m.c. a come-hither look as she passes. The m.c., taking the bait, begins to follow her off stage. At that moment, a homosexual soldier enters stage left. He minces across the stage, making the same sexual overtures as the gal. The m.c., by this time is halfway off stage following the gal. He stops suddenly, looks at the pansy, looks back at the gal, then turns and follows the pansy offstage. (Rim-shot.)

On and on went the skits. To pull it all off we had the wonderful Bill Rizos as m.c. He was a fast-talking kid from eastern Pennsylvania, with a high-powered personality and a good comedic sense. He told a joke for his opening monologue. It went like this:

Men are at a park playing softball. The team at bat is one man short. They recruit a young black boy to fill-in. He protests that he doesn't know how to play baseball, but they push him toward the plate to take his turn at bat. Just hit the ball with the bat, his teammates tell him. This he does with a powerful wallop, and the ball sails out of the park for a home run. "Run, Willie, run, they scream at him, "run round those bases, Willie, run, run."

"Run, hell," Willie replies, "I'll buy 'em a new ball." (Rim shot.)

There was a soldier in C Battery, a strange young man, short and heavy set. He was called only by his last name, Younger. (I believe his first name was Ted). He was on a gun crew. He did his job quietly and kept to himself. We knew very little about him, for he shared no personal information with us. We did know one thing, though; he had a showbiz background. Rumors had circulated that he and his parents were part of a circus act or a vaudeville act. But whatever his actual background was, it was obvious that he was a showbiz pro. I didn't come into contact with him often, but on those occasions when we were together, he seemed morose and withdrawn. But when we heard good news, news, for example, about the outfit getting a pass or being granted a furlough or going home or shooting down a JU-88 — almost anything good — Younger wouldn't smile or utter a sound, but would immediately show his pleasure by going into a soft-shoe dance, neither his heavy boots nor the rough terrain being any impediment. You could tell immediately from the grace of his movements that he was a great dancer, that you were watching a real pro in action.

Younger's companion through the war was his mandolin, which he played frequently. Some of the men in C Battery swear they once heard him play "Flight of the Bumblebee." So with a talented guy like Younger, we thought we were sure to have a socko show. I'd even gone so far as to schedule him to do a fast tap for the show opener. I also thought he might do a mandolin solo midway in the show and then reprise with the tap number as a closer. The only hitch was that no one had contacted him. When he was finally approached, however, he refused to appear. He didn't equivocate. He didn't explain. He just gave us a flat out no. It mystified us, and to this day I can't understand why he refused.

In spite of Younger's absence, we had a pretty fair show. We entertained our own men, then took the show on the road — a few miles away to a Corps of Engineers outfit. It looked like we had a hit. Our next booking was at an army hospital, several miles away. It was our most important booking, and we prepared for it conscientiously. At showtime, we gave it everything we had, and the nurses in the audience responded enthusiastically, laughing uproariously at every gag. Midway in the show, however, a colonel in the Medical Corps came out of the audience and held up both hands. "I'm sorry," he said. "this show is closed. The material is indecent and not suitable for anybody, especially the young women in the audience."

Backstage, we heard the audience groan. We could scarcely believe what had happened. Not suitable for young women? Holy shit! These same young women knew every part of the male anatomy, had washed and cleaned the wounded, assisted in operating on them and had shaved the pubic hair around their penises before surgery. The show folded on the spot. We never put on another one.

It turned out that the offending skit was the one about the homosexual. It had been our biggest laugh-getter. Back then, nearly fifty-five years ago, the skit was regarded as offensive because it was concerned with what then was regarded as a perversion. It's ironic, but the same skit wouldn't play today either, but on the grounds of political correctness.

Charlie and Nita live in a modest but comfortable home. She is a deeply religious woman. He, on the other hand, can take religion or leave it alone, but lately her proselytizing efforts have begun to pay off, and Charlie admits to have been "semi-converted." He is an accepting person. He has come to terms with his leukemia and with his depleted income. "Financial considerations," he says, are the reason he hasn't attended all our reunions.

"I wish we were living in simpler times," he said, as I sat with him in his living room.

I nodded.

"The world was so much better then, wasn't it Charlie?"

He brushed off my question as if no answer were necessary.

Before I ended my visit, Charlie asked that I sit down on the couch for a moment.

"What's up?" I asked.

"Shut up and listen," he said.

He walked over to the piano, looked down at the keyboard, then threw me a glance. There was a twinkle in his eye.

He played three numbers for me — "Holiday for Strings," "I Should Care" and "Dream."

By the time he had finished I had tears in my eyes. I continued sitting on the couch, unwilling to break my reverie.

Finally, I got up to leave, took out my handkerchief and wiped my eyes. We shook hands, the melodies still swirling in my head.

Charlie looked at me sympathetically.

"The 124th is a major part of my life, too," he said, consolingly.

"I know, Charlie," I said.

We shook hands, and I bid goodbye to Nita. I walked out of the house, got into my car and headed for Tulsa.

FOURTEEN

As I drove toward Tulsa, I thought about the weeks I had spent in Oklahoma researching, *Jews Among The Indians,* a book I had written in 1992. It was understandable that thoughts of the Indians would enter my mind, and most especially those of Chief Samuel Checote, who lived during the middle of the nineteenth century and was part of the Indian world of that territory. I admit it's a bit strange to have as a hero a man I had never known or seen outside the pages of a rare history book, but he shares a place in my galaxy of idols right alongside Dutch Reagan and Carl Hubbell.

After driving awhile I left Cherokee territory, where Talequah is located, and entered the lands once belonging to the Creek nation. I had spent several days there — in Tulsa, Muscogee and Okmulgee, and it was familiar territory. I remember coming away marked by a sadness that I doubt will ever leave me. The source was the shameful condition of the burial site of Samuel Checote, that old Indian chief whose life had left such a strong imprint on me.

In 1869, the Creeks elected Checote as their principal chief. He was tall, well-educated, a soft-spoken Confederate army hero, a man in striking contrast to the popular notion of what Indians are really like. To Ulysses S. Grant, Checote was "the greatest Indian I have ever met."

Checote enlisted in the Confederate army in August, 1861, entering as a captain of company B, First Regiment, Creek

Mounted Volunteers, and within the year had been promoted to Lt. Colonel. His Creek regiment, while a part of the First Indian Cavalry Brigade of the Confederate army, attacked a federal supply train between Fort Scott, Kansas, a Union supply depot, and Fort Gibson, Oklahoma. The train was made up of 300 wagons carrying military supplies as well as supplies for settlers and traders. Goods and military equipment were valued at $1.5 million. Checote's capture of the supply train was a tremenduous boost to the Confederate cause.

I had spent time going through some of Checote's papers at the Oklahoma State Archives, and developed a special interest in this unusual man who some of the old Indians, according to historian O.A. Lambert, still speak of today as their great chief, "gentle as a child, courageous as a lion, whose life left an impress on his people for good more than all other chiefs in their history."

I was so impressed with Checote that at the time I decided to drive to Okmulgee, the capital of the Creek nation, to visit the chief's grave. I remember having driven down the main street of Okmulgee looking for the headquarters of the Creek nation. It was located in the center of town, a gray stone building set inside a small courtyard. I asked the Indians inside if anyone knew the whereabouts of Samuel Checote's grave. The Indians shook their heads. One Indian woman said that a descendant of Checote lived in Okmulgee, and might be able to help. She made a telephone call, but the relative also didn't know. I thanked the Indians and walked out. As I passed through the courtyard, I saw a marker erected by the Oklahoma Historical Society, which lauded Chief Checote and gave directions to his gravesite. I couldn't understand it. The Indians at Creek headquarters had to pass the marker each day yet none was aware of what was printed on it.

I followed directions on the plaque to the outskirts of town, and pulled my car up to the Newtown Methodist Church. It was located on a country road, a well-kept white frame building. No one was on the premises. I walked to the back of the church, where off in the distance I spotted a sign, written in the Creek language, designating the site as an Indian burial ground. I could see nothing more than an empty field covered over with a century old growth of weeds and underbrush. Somewhere out in that field were the remains of a great war hero, the greatest Indian Ulysses Grant had ever met.

I recall leaving the burial ground shaking my head in dismay. Checote's accomplishments in trying to protect the integrity of Indian lands, as well as his heroism during the Civil War, had been forgotten, wiped out as surely as though he had never existed. To the chief, virtue, I surmise, may have been its own reward, but for his admirers who may have wanted to offer a tribute it was a disappointment. More important, for the current and future generation of Indians who could derive a sense of pride from knowing about the old Indian, the lack of a monument, even a modest headstone, to mark his life, is to deprive them of a sense of their noble heritage.

I must confess that I had also felt a sadness for myself as well as for all the men and women who had served in all our wars, warriors who were destined to be forgotten. Most of us are merely imperceptible blips on history's screen, but even a blip deserves a marker, some designation that they had once inhabited the earth, had served their time and had moved on. Checote deserved at least that, and a whole lot more.

In thinking about Checote's burial site, my mind turned to my father. He had survived World War I and is buried in Des Moines, in the Jewish section of Glendale cemetery, a discreet distance apart from the graves of my mother and her family. There was no money to bury him, for no one had come forth with the money to do it. It was only through the intervention of the Jewish War Veterans that he had an appropriate burial, the expense for both the burial and the military headstone marking his grave having been paid for by veterans like himself. My mother and her family may not have chosen to acknowledge his existence but the Jewish War Veterans did, and I am indebted to them.

I visit my father's grave on occasion. His fellow veterans, for many years, had placed a small American flag on his headstone every Memorial Day. The site is strewn with weeds, and you can tell it receives only minimal care. But, yes, it's a marker, and when I stand before it I begin to reflect on a whole range of matters that I might have not confronted if there had been no marker to signal his presence, some object to which I can address my questions or which, as it once had been, an object to receive my tears.

I stand before the old man and speak to him. I ask this buried body why he had never once come to see his son, his only child, a subject on which my mother was mute until the day she died. I ask him if he had ever felt remorse in having abandoned me and if he hadn't, what sort of a man could he have been to have been so indifferent. I want him to supply me with some justification for his actions. Was there some denial of visitation rights in my parents' divorce degree, some threat of exposure if he came to see me? Or what other reasons could there have been — a personal humiliation of some kind; a blinding hatred of my mother or my mother's hatred of him? I exhaust all the possibilities, hoping that I can settle on one, even one, which seems reasonable. But so far I haven't been able to. Of all these seemingly plausible explanations, the one I live with is that he simply didn't want to see me; it's as simple as that. Otherwise why wouldn't he have cast aside whatever external restraints there may have been and come to see me anyway, no matter what the consequences, just as I would do if I had been in his shoes.

So I stand over his headstone and look down on his grave, confronting and re-confronting the issue, addressing a silent person with questions that just might evoke an answer if asked often enough, or that, best of all, may finally produce a body rising up from the grave, shouting: "Enough already with the questions — here's the truth..."

Surely, if there was a marker for Checote's grave, the young Indians would have questions to put to the old chief, too, questions which must be equally as perplexing as my own.

Often I hear people say that when their time comes they'd like to be cremated and have their ashes strewn here or there — on a golf course, in the ocean, at Disneyland, or on the spot where their raspberry plants grow. In my view, it's arrogant and cynical, depriving survivors of a place to pay tribute, to declare their love or air their disputes. Want to pay your respects to your old man? Hell, just walk out on the fairway of that par five water hole, and while you're at it bring your clubs. Want to pay your respects to Chief Checote? — go stand somewhere in that field and bow down before a clump of underbrush.

When the 124th held its fiftieth reunion in Riverside, it was on the site of what was then Camp Haan, now an army cemetery. The grounds are immaculately groomed. The crosses and Stars of David are recessed in the form of flat tablets, and in this way the groundskeepers can cut the lawn without having to work around the upright grave markers. It is an impressive resting place, and it is where I choose to be buried. It not only is on the site of my original army camp, but on the cemetery wall is a plaque dedicated to the 124th and noting the site as our original training camp. It is the most appropriate place I can think of to be buried, but in addition its location is my beloved California, less than an hour's drive from Sunset and Vine where I used to walk with Anita. It is a place where my children and grandchildren can come to visit the old man, just as I do in Des Moines with my old man.

I had arranged to meet John Behl and his wife, Marilouise, for dinner in Tulsa that evening. John had been a first lieutenant in C Battery. I didn't remember him from the war, but as he had been a regular reunion goer over the years, I'd had the opportunity to strike up a close friendship with him later on. John planned to pick me up at the Ramada Inn near the airport where I'd be staying for the night. He and Marilouise were right on time when they arrived. We drove to one of their favorite haunts, an Irish Pub where the martinis were generous, the food good. Trust John to have the inside track on the good things in life. A big, warm-hearted fellow, he is an affable companion, drinking or not, and I feel genuinely at ease in his company. John was then on the hard side of 75, a quiet go-along kind of man who bears none of the pretensions of once having been an officer. It's difficult to imagine that with his slightly high-pitched voice and his unassertiveness that he had barked out orders to the troops and made them snap-to. At the business meetings which are a part of every reunion, John sits quietly with Marilouise, never making a comment, leaving the talking to Ed Soares and Bo Smith. Even though rank no longer means a damn in the 124th, there is a noticeable difference in tone in the way the men address John Behl. He commands a great deal of respect, and it's not just because he was once an officer but because of the kind of man he is.

Over drinks, John gave me an account of his career. He had graduated from the University of Arkansas in 1940. Earlier, in 1938, he joined Oklahoma Tire and Supply, at its satellite operation in Carthage, Missouri, at a monthly salary of 35 dollars.

"I came with five bucks in my pocket," he recalled.

The firm, which later came to be known as Otasco, was founded by the Sanditen brothers, three Jewish boys, Maurice, Henry and Sam. Two of the brothers lived in Okmulgee which was then the heart of the firm's business. Within a year John was promoted to assistant manager of the Carthage operation.

He enlisted in the air corps December 5, 1941, two days before Pearl Harbor.

"When I was called, I refused to go," he said.

"Did you turn chicken, John?"

"Hell, no," he said, "I couldn't go because I had to take inventory."

When he was finally called up he spent eleven months in the air corps band and was finally transfered to Officers Candidate School in the Coast Artillery Corps, the forerunner of Anti-Aircraft, at Camp Davis, North Carolina. Eventually he was transfered to the 124th.

The war over, he rejoined Otasco for a few years, but switched gears in 1948 to become a principal with Tiffin Teeter, a florist operation in Carthage. When he subsequently sold the flower shop, he returned once more to Otasco, this time as senior vice-president, where he remained until his retirement.

Sometime earlier, I had sent John a copy of my book knowing of his Oklahoma background. As we talked it seemed doubly appropriate that I had done so because of his long standing involvement with Otasco and the Sanditen brothers, the Okmulgee Jews.

I told John of some of my experiences in Muscogee and my disappointment in finding Samuel Checote's grave in shambles. He was well acquainted with Muscogee. He nodded in agreement when I sang the praises of the chicken fried steak which I had found to be the most noteworthy hallmark of the town. He was not familiar with Samuel Checote. I wouldn't have expected him to be. No one else is either, the Indians included.

I was matching John martini for martini while Marilouise listened dutifully, sipping her own drink.

He has been attending reunions since 1968. I asked him if he thought we had many left to hold now that Ed Harris wasn't around to prod us.

"There aren't many of us left," I said. "And those of us still alive aren't in good shape."

"That makes it even more important that we continue to have them," he said, firmly.

"That's so."

I recall that I wanted to ask him whether he had plans for his own burial. Was he as preoccupied with death as I was? Was he

"I have two sons and three grand-children," he said, "but the men of the 124th, they're my family ties. I have no brothers or sisters."

headed for a military cemetery, say the one in Riverside? Well, those are questions you just don't blurt out, no matter how close you feel to someone. In any case, John is the kind of company you'd want in any burial ground, a real solid guy who enjoys his martinis.

"I have two sons and three grandchildren," he said, "but the men of the 124th —- they're my family ties. I have no brothers or sisters."

"I'm in exactly the same boat," I said. "Much as I love them, I can't relate to my own sons in the way I can with you and some of the others."

"Of course not, the young people don't care. They don't speak our language, and anything's okay with them if they don't have to pay. Aw, what the hell," he said, finally, "the country's going down the tube anyway."

FIFTEEN

I had never been quite as lonely as during the summer months of training at Camp Irwin, California, the desert firing range. Civilization, which by my definition then was a cold bottle of beer and a public telephone from which I could call Anita, was located in Barstow, 35 miles to the south. There was nothing else in any direction except desert wasteland. Somewhere to the north, however, was Death Valley, a place I had only read about and knew as well as the locale of the old radio show. I can still hear the announcer as he slowly drawled out the name of the show, *Death Valley Days*, in a tone that managed to capture the dry, dust-bitten voice of a lonely old prospector. I was fascinated by the aura of this desert outpost— as nature's worst hell-hole where only the heartiest of men continuously waged battle against sand and thirst, only in the end to fall prey to the savage appetite of the circling vulture. Twenty-Mule Team Borax was the sponsor of the show. The product, whose properties, uses and benefits were never clearly explained, was as mysterious as Death Valley itself, seemingly having achieved some consumer success by conjuring up an image of sun-parched old desert rats carrying glittering nuggets in their saddlebags. These same perceptions of both product and locale were mind-gripping during my days at Camp Irwin. I would stare out across the desert believing that Death Valley was out there close at hand, perhaps just over some sand-covered mound and not, as I later discovered it to be, nearly 100 miles due north, as the crow flies.

My attraction to Death Valley, indeed to the entire state of California, had not yet been fully satisfied when I decided to make a trip there in 1994. The conditions were that I wanted to run through the Valley in August, the hottest of three torturously hot summer months. I had just turned 70 the previous month, and I not only wanted to engage in a test of endurance with Father Time but to pit myself as well against blistering heat, one of the cruelest forces of nature. The floor of the valley lies 250-feet below sea level, where the midday temperature hovers between 120-and 130-degrees. I figured that if I could run three-miles a day at high noon and then hike an additional three miles, I could lay claim to whatever Victory Cup is awarded to foolish old men who are trying to prove they're fitter than younger men.

As a fastidious planner, I first called the ranger station to find out where to stay and what provisions to bring. After listening to my questions, an impatient ranger advised me to forego any plans to run but rather to try to take a slow leisurely walk after sundown, an alternative to running that would tax, the ranger said, even the fittest of us. Under any conditions he advised me to carry four quarts of water, adding that they will be empty in less than an hour. It was advice I quickly rejected. To carry one quart, fine — two quarts, possibly; but four quarts would have been out of the question unless I was to have a burro jogging along beside me. Despite the ranger's warnings, I was still not deterred. I was going to run through Death Valley no matter what.

There are two places to stay in the Valley. One is an expensive spot called Furnace Creek Lodge which is closed during the summer, the other a much less expensive lodge, built along the lines of an army barracks, where there is a restaurant, a concession stand and a gas station. During the summer it affords lodging and refreshments to bus loads of German and French tourists who seem to thrive on the scenery of the American West and especially on the stifling heat. The Europeans are dead giveaways, easily identifiable even without opening their mouths. They are attired in shorts and wear sandals over heavy woolen socks and seem to be emulating the look, in the Germans' case, of their fathers and grandfathers who served with Field Marshall Rommel in the Afrika Corps. The few Americans who come to the Valley during the summer wear sandals or sneakers and, perish the thought, socks of even the lightest of cottons.

In planning the trip, I decided not to stay in the Valley itself but to find a motel in Beatty, Nevada, 20 miles away, and to commute to the Valley each morning. I also decided to first head for Fresno, California, and then double back to Death Valley. I wanted to spend some time with Earl White, another reunion addict, who had been quite ill in recent years and unable to travel. I phoned to tell him I was coming to Fresno to see him before flying to Death Valley. He seemed delighted because we hadn't seen each other in a few years. Even though we had very little contact during the war, we became fast friends at some of our earlier reunions. I first got to know him during the show we staged in Germany. Earl was in the band playing the bass drums. He was later demoted to playing cymbals because, as he himself likes to admit, "I was always half-a-beat off."

In order to visit Earl, I first had to fly to San Francisco and then await a crop duster to get me down to Fresno. When I arrived in Fresno, I rented a car and drove to a motel that Earl had recommended, located just off Blackstone avenue, where prostitutes saunter boldly down the street in the dark hours. Or so said Earl.

After I checked in, I drove over to Shield street where Earl and his wife lived. In my eagerness to see him I had nearly forgotten that Earl was a very sick man who had suffered from cancer for a number of years. He had had at least three cancer operations that I was aware of and had been surviving on an extended series of chemotherapy treatments and radiation therapy. He had lost weight since I last saw him, and his once shiny black hair looked like desert scruff. God love him, he hadn't lost his sense of humor.

"Sure took you a long time getting here," he said. "I'll bet you stopped off on Blackstone for a quickie."

"Now, Earl..."

I leaned over and gave him a kiss on the forehead.

"No lip-kissing," he said, waving a warning finger.

"It's going to be hard to resist," I said.

He was sitting at the dining room table, doing some writing and drawing.

"Here, this is for you."

He reached across the table and handed me one of his pictures, an ink drawing of the skeleton of a fish, neatly framed. He had titled it, "Death Valley Trout."

"Earl, you're too much. I'll cherish this."

I was touched by the gift and by the neat bit of irony, and he knew it.

"Now don't start doing a Hank Stefani on me."

"What do you mean?"

"You know Hank?"

"Sure I know Hank," I said.

"Hank would cry at the drop of a hat, didn't you know that?"

"I guess not."

"Well, he would. Whenever he said goodbye to anybody, he'd start bawling. Once at a reunion, he slobbered all over me and gave me a big kiss on the lips."

"I haven't seen Hank in a while," I said unhappily.

"I know. He hasn't been coming to the reunions lately."

"What happened? He was one of the early gang."

"I don't know," he said, "he got pissed off at someone. Or at something. I'm not sure which."

I could tell that he wasn't giving me the whole story.

"So go ahead, finish."

"That's about it," said Earl, "I told you he was an emotional guy."

Hank Stefani is a short, wiry man who wears a lot of metal around his neck. My recollection is that he came from somewhere in the Bay area and was in the retail grocery business with his brothers. At each reunion, Hank would tell me about a new chapter in his life, like telling me he had moved to Placerville, California, a strange decision for a guy like Hank who I'd always judged to have a big city sharpness about him. Then another time, more recently, he told me had moved to a small town in Idaho. I called him a few years ago to talk. He's a sweet guy, and I miss him. I didn't ask why he had settled in Idaho, or why he was repudiating the counsel of Horace Greeley by continually heading east — or for that matter why he hadn't attended reunions during the past few years. In any case, he was happy to hear from me, and urged me to come out for a visit. He wanted me to stay with him, and would have it no other way.

Back in Fresno, Earl is one of these guys whose features are puzzling. You can't figure out exactly what his origins are, and I've never bothered to ask. Instead, I've played a guessing game with myself for many years and had just about concluded that he was some sort of an exotic mongrel. He is a tall man with jet black hair (in his pre-chemotherapy days) and very dark skin, as dark as any Afro-American. Yet his features are roman, his speech uncontaminated by any trace of regional or foreign influences. It was not until my visit with him that he disclosed in passing that he was of Portuguese ancestry. It cleared up a mystery but was not a matter worth commenting on. Instead, I nodded knowingly, and at the same time mentioned, in some context or other, my Jewish background. My being Jewish was, of course, a fact well known

He was a very sick man who had been surviving on an extended series of chemotherapy treatments. "I miss all the guys. I love them," he said, turning his head away. "If I could only see them one more time."

throughout the battalion. I also mentioned gratuitously that I was the only Jew in the battalion.

As soon as I spoke, he bolted upright in his chair.

"What did you say?"

"I said, Earl, that I was the only Jew in the battalion."

"The hell you were."

"What are you talking about?" I sputtered.

"You were not the only Jew," he said firmly. Actually, there may have been two others."

"Now I know you're full of shit," I said.

"No, no," he protested, "why would I make something like that up."

"Because you're a perverse sonofabitch," I said, "and you're trying to rob me of any claim I have of being unique."

"Right hand up, I'm not kidding."

"Name 'em," I said.

"I can't name the second one, but one was definitely Bill Meltzer in C Battery."

"Meltzer?" I said. "I don't believe it. You mean the guy who was in the show with us?"

"Yep."

"Meltzer?" I repeated.

"Yep."

The news was shocking. For years I would tell anyone who'd listen that I was the battalion's only Jew, and it was hard for them to imagine that I could endure such hardship. I could imagine them thinking: in addition to doing battle with the Nazis, this poor fellow was locked in a solitary struggle against anti-Semitism, continually being berated, called kike, sheeney and Christ-killer by his comrades and yet managing to survive the war in one piece, his hide untarnished by either enemy, the one within or the one without. I relished their sympathy. I read it in their downcast eyes and in the pitying shake of their heads. But now what? If Earl was right and if Meltzer truly was a Jew and not some fractionated species of Jew, I would be forced to share all this sympathy — half of it now going to Meltzer instead of all of it to me. As an only child, I am not, suffice it to say, very big on sharing.

Earl has had an interesting career. He has been a clothing salesman and a jewelry salesman, and for 32 years had been employed by Pacific Bell. Along the line, he became a Union Steward and then Chief Steward of the Communication Workers of America. He was the CWA's legislative representative, and once had his picture taken with Jimmy Carter, that photo being a matter of considerable pride. He does not hesitate in owning up to the fact that he was a fuckup in the army, citing his record of having been busted from pfc to private 11 different times.

No one will argue that Earl is a big man in the San Joachin Valley. He was a Cub Scoutmaster and Boy Scoutmaster, and was voted Toastmaster of the Year by the Toastmaster Club of Central California.

"Not bad," he said, "for a timid Portuguese kid."

Earl and his wife, Sallie, a WAC during the war, have three children. One son, a twin, died a few years ago. When he feels up to it, Earl spends his free time fishing.

"I miss all the guys. I love them." And then, pausing and turning his head away. he said, "If I could only see them one more time."

I looked at his frail body, a body punished by chemicals and radiation and the effects of three operations. I put my hand on his hand.

"You will, Earl," I assured him.

I kissed him goodbye and headed for the door on my way to Death Valley.

Beatty, Nevada, is a small desert community, totally without charm, which seemingly sprang up out of nowhere. There are no houses, only mobile homes; no sidewalks or paved sidestreets, only two highways bisecting each other. There are three or four motels, several gas stations, a grocery store and a brothel.

My motel was quite adequate, better than I had anticipated. It had an adjoining restaurant and bar, and several slot machines. At night I drank, played Video Poker at a quarter a shot, and usually wound up the evening by walking across the highway to a Shell station for a candy bar. It was a surprisingly peaceful time.

On my first trip into Death Valley I realized that I should have stayed in Fresno and hung out a few days longer with Earl. A sudden encounter with the heat in the Valley stunned me in my tracks, cut off my breathing and rendered me useless for any physical exertion. I was drained of stamina, drained of motivation. I wanted to find some shade and drink an ice-cold beer instead of duking it out with Mother Nature. Still, I was determined to carry on with my idea. I checked in at the Ranger station when I arrived, now more as a cowering old man than as a fire-eating warrior. With a taste of the heat under my belt I now became willing to heed the warnings of the ranger.

There is a frontage trail with a macadam surface alongside the highway. It begins at the ranger station and extends past the barracks-like lodge, past the gas station, for about a mile or more. It is an ideal running surface, and I decided to make that my indoctrination run. I stashed half of my water supply in my car; and still continuing to fight-on, I began my run. I moved out slowly at first, for this had been my plan. But after the first few yards, I began to sag under the weight of my two canteens, my breathing coming in short gasps, my legs like dead weights, failing to respond to the brain's messages. Fight-on, old-timer, fight on, the messages seemed to say. But after the first 200 yards, the signals grew weaker. I had no choice but to turn around and walk back to the lodge. I was a loser, a failure. I bought a coke and sat down, exhausted.

I watched as an air-conditioned tour bus pulled in to the lodge and emptied out its cargo of rosy-cheeked smiling Europeans. I stared at their sandals and heavy woolen socks as they alighted from the bus. They were baby-boomers — clerks and school teachers and librarians, many were women. Their faces were bright with anticipation, their eyes wide with wonder. But then abruptly their expressions changed, their faces now turned grim, and I knew they had suddenly felt the first deadly rush of the heat. At that moment, I sensed they would have traded it all in for a cool afternoon in a *bier stube,* as I would have done, as any old man would have done who has finally realized that the fight was over, that the only choice left was to grow old gracefully.

There was a book waiting for me when I returned to Chicago, a dog-eared copy of a half-century old volume titled *Loafing Through Death Valley.* Earl had sent it to me. He had evidently found it in a second-hand book store. I haven't gotten around to reading it yet. I don't know, maybe I never will.

SIXTEEN

In World War II films, Hollywood gave its characters nick-names like "Brooklyn" (fast-talking, dark-haired sharpies) or "Alabama" (sweet, innocent, slow talking types). But there were no such stereotypes in the 124th. We had no one from Brooklyn, and there was just a handful of men from the Gulf states. The men from California and Texas, on the other hand, acccounted for nearly half the battalion, and among this group, Mexican-Americans were a dominant force. On the whole they were good men and good soldiers. And while many were sweet and fun-loving, others were mean-eyed bandidos with chips on their shoulders who liked to drink and scrap in the local bars. When they got drunk and began to fight, they came looking for protection from Jim Oxford who also drank and scrapped. "Help me, Jeem," they would plead, and Jim with his dukes up would hide them behind his big frame.

In combat, we fired our big 90-millimeter guns from huge bunkers, dug deep enough for a six-footer to stand up in, lined bottom to top with sandbags, and covered over with camouflage netting. It was no place for men with delicate sensibilities. The recoil of the guns could jar an elephant herd and the sound of the exploding shells was as ear-shattering as the obscenities uttered by the Mexicans on the gun crews. *A la chingada* would come the cry. *Cono* someone would say, and back would come *Chinga tu madre*. Or *esto me jode* (I'm sick and tired of this fucking shit.) Sounds of soldiers in battle. Sounds from a Phoenix bunker...

Until my mother and I had moved to Phoenix I had never

seen a Mexican, never heard one speak. All at once I was exposed to a barrage of epithets I'd never heard before. It took me no time at all to learn the words, *mala palabras,* bad words, words that weren't taught in my first year Spanish class at Phoenix Union High. I recall walking home from school one blistering hot September afternoon. The streets were deserted except for a few students on their way home and a few of the city's elderly. The older folks walked slowly, holding umbrellas to block out the sun, always wary of heat stroke. The students wore the prescribed uniform, sweat stained T-shirts and dirty Levis.

When I reached 3rd Street and Roosevelt, I spotted a couple of Mexican laborers working in a bunker, evidently repairing sewers. They were naked from the waist up and wore red bandanas on their heads. Their bodies, nearly black from the sun, glistened with sweat. I felt sorry for them, working so hard under a sweltering sun. They had little to look forward to when they finished work except to return to their crowded shacks somewhere south of Buckeye Road, only to get drunk on beer and swelter some more. This was before air-conditioning, and while we Anglos also suffered from the heat, the Mexicans lived with their families in very crowded quarters which made matters far worse for them.

Even at the tender age of 14, I felt obliged to speak to the workers as I walked by.

"Hola, esta mucho color," I said in my best freshman Spanish.

"Fawk you, said one of the men, an evil grin distorting his face, his eyes smoldering with hatred. *"Chinga tu madre."*

Sounds from a Phoenix bunker.

I continued walking, not daring to look back in case they wanted to hop up out of their bunker and beat me up. It wasn't until I reached Pierce street, a block farther north, that I had the courage to look back. At the time, I was hurt and confused by their display of hatred. But that was before I learned about poverty and anger, about gringos and Mexicans, about the haves and the have-nots of the world.

It was as combat soldiers that our Mexican comrades earned my admiration. One of them, Marcellino Matamoros, remained in the army and rose to the rank of Master Sergeant. The last time I saw him was at our reunion in Reno in the mid-1980's. He was resplendent in his full dress uniform with ribbons plastered all over his tunic. He was lean, mean and tough, rail-thin and ramrod straight, Government Issue from his head down to his spit-shined boots. He had seen action in Korea and Viet Nam in addition to World War II. I continue to stand in awe of spit and polish professional soldiers like Marcellino, their shirts bearing three razor sharp creases, each as sharp as any knife they may have had tucked away in their pockets.

I often think about my Mexican brothers, their names and faces flashing before me to this day. Of course, I think about Phil

I recall that he sat quietly, content within himslef, smiling at the laughter and hijinx at the table, but never joining in. Despite his quite demeanor, down deep he was a tough hombre, a professional warrior who re-enlisted when the 124th broke up after VE-day. He eventually rose to 1st Sergeant in the infantry while serving in Korea.

Rodriguez, and always will. I also think about the others I served with, most of whom are dead. There were the Martinez's — Pifanio, Rubel, Tony, Catarfino, and E. F. all five of them unrelated. And there was Frank Jiminez, Pedro Salinas, Jose Servey, Macario Reyna, Elroy Avila, Eliazar Camarillo, Pete Garza, Frank Cisneros, Manuel Villanueva, Julio Fernades, Guadalupe Villarreal, Santos Rangel, Juan Saucedo, Camarino Dias, Frank Sanchez, Guillermo Mascias and Ysabel Contreras.

There were at least three of these men who gave me a hard time. They guyed and joked when my back was turned, and when I turned to confront them I was met with their mean hard-eyed stares, as if to say *"no me jodas,"* don't fuck with us, or else. I never learned the reason for their hatred. Maybe it was because I represented all the cocky punk Anglos in their lives. Or maybe it was because I was one of the hated *rico Israelitos,* rich Jews. That all Jews were rich was, and still is, a common misconception, but if that was the source of their hostility they had the wrong soldier. My experience with poverty was as broad and miserable as their own.

Ysabel Contreras was a friend. He was known to every one as Pancho. No one dared call him Ysabel, but if you did you pronounced his name correctly, as ee-sa-bell, and not as iz-a-bell. He was assigned to D Battery as a range technician, and hence he was not on a gun crew. Because I was in A Battery, I can't remember ever seeing him in Europe. In later years I saw him at our reunions, and we merely nodded to each other, never speaking. He is a pleasant, heavy-set man who keeps to himself, smiles easily but is not an active socializer. In that way he is different from the other more boisterous Mexicans in the battalion. In our earlier reunion days there was no sign of Pancho among any of the men hanging out in the hotel bars. In fact, I wouldn't have known he was in attendance if I hadn't seen him sitting by himself in the hotel lobbies or having breakfast, often alone, in the hotel restaurants. Throughout the years, our acquaintanceship still continued but only on a nodding basis. I didn't know his name, and I don't think he knew mine. I had heard the name, "Pancho Contreras" in one context or another but I didn't know that the quiet man I had seen for so many years was *the* Pancho Contreras.

A few times I had found myself at the same table with Pancho at our Saturday night banquets. I recall that he sat quietly, content within himself, smiling at the laughter and hijinx at the table, but never joining in. At the time I had him figured as a deeply wounded man who had had some tough breaks in life. Despite his quiet demeanor down deep he was a tough hombre, a professional warrior who re-enlisted when the 124th broke up after V-E day. He eventually rose to 1st Sergeant in the Infantry, while serving in Korea.

After I said goodbye to Earl White, I had some time before I was due at the Fresno airport. I stopped at a pay phone and called Pancho in Silvis, a sister community of Fresno. I caught up with him at work. I explained who I was and why I wanted to see him. He invited me to come to a Peach street address. It was on a residential street, a modest home with an adjoining garage. When I arrived, the door to the garage was open. Several women sat around a long table in the garage, making pottery; some were Anglos, some Mexican. A pleasant looking Anglo woman, seated at the head of the table, greeted me with a cordial smile as I walked in. It was evidently her residence and it was she who was conducting the pottery-making class. I told her I had come to see Pancho. She turned and called out to him.

I felt some trepidation about seeing him, having no idea what to expect. Here was a fellow I had never made the effort to talk with, nor had he with me. Furthermore, I had a fear of the potential violence of some of the Mexicans, remembering the time during the war when Snake's bayonet was pointed at my jugular. I also haven't forgotten how one of the Mexican laborers in Phoenix had inexplicably erupted in anger at my greeting. As for Pancho, he was a mystery man. I really didn't know him, and wondered if he might take offense at some of my questions and unexpectedly turn mean.

Any such fears were unfounded. When he saw me, he greeted me with a big smile and guided me through the garage, past where the women were making pottery, and then through a side door into the kitchen. He seemed to have full run of the place, and it wouldn't have been a surprise if he told me he lived there permanently, with the lady of the house being more than a mere employer.

After we were seated at the kitchen table, he asked if he could get me anything to eat or drink. I shook my head, and we began to talk about Earl. Pancho knew that Earl had cancer, but it was clear that the two men weren't close, even though they lived near each other.

Most of the men in the battalion talk about their troubles with officers during the war. Pancho was no exception, but what I found interesting is that he made no attempt to explain who the officers were and what his beef was. Had he done so, I would have been surprised. That wouldn't have been his style.

His army history was heroic and varied. While I'm sure he had been decorated, he made no mention of it. He had been an MP attached to the 26th infantry, and later served in the Tank Corps in Korea. He fought at Pork Chop Hill, the last major engagement of the Korean War.

In civilian life, his career was fascinating and equally varied. After he was mustered out of service he went to work for a local manufacturing company as a machinist, retiring at 64. He had been employed by the same company for 43 years. He now works part-time as a security guard and as a part-time helper in the ceramics studio.

Earlier, he spent a lot of time on the baseball scene, just as Ed Harris had. He organized and managed a girls' softball team in the Valley, and at one point, as the manager of a Little League team, had Tom Seaver, the Yankee ace, on his roster. In addition, he himself had played pro ball for the San Francisco Seals and had a stint as a professional boxer, fighting as a bantam weight. As a professional bowler, he maintains a 202 average.

His wife died in 1959, but I didn't get the impression that he's a lonely man, despite his being a loner. He has three dogs and a lot of kids and grandkids. I doubt that he has many friends, no matter that he is a long-time resident of the San JoachinValley.

He was not hesitant about opening up to me, but I sensed that any questions I might ask about his relationship with his lady employer, even in a roundabout way, would be seriously off limits. He spoke lovingly about his affection for the men in the battalion, especially for Ed Harris. He recalled that Ed, at the time of our reunion in Vancouver, Washington, had driven up from L.A., had stopped for him in Fresno, and had then driven him to Vancouver and back, just as he had done for Phil Rodriguez. He wasn't curious about me, about the book or about my family. Although he asked no questions of me, he politely responded to those I asked him. We shook hands when I said goodbye, and we both promised to stay in touch.

I saw Pancho again at a reunion in Las Vegas. Two years had gone by since I visited him in Silvis. I noticed that he still kept to himself, and was never in the company of any of the other men. I saw him eating alone in the hotel restaurant, and passed him several times in the hotel casino. As was our history, we spoke not a word. We knew we didn't have to. We nodded to each other, of course, and that was enough.

SEVENTEEN

It is late afternoon in Scottsdale. I am lying on the bed in my motel room, thinking that it's time to get up and get dressed for the reunion banquet. This is our 54th reunion, 54 chicken dinners, thousands of rolls of film, hundreds of faces swirling around. And memories — too many to flesh out. Several of the men I had last seen, either in their home towns or at our Vegas reunion a few years before, had not come to Scottsdale. John Behl, Phil Rodriguez and Earl White were gone, but what about Jim Oxford, Pancho Contreras, Dean Calico and Paul Heiser — where the hell were they anyway?

I shower and get dressed and head for the lobby. The banquet is held in a room adjacent to the swimming pool. The tables are arranged in a semi-circle around a small dance floor. The cash bar, where men once stood three deep waiting for service, is off in a far corner of the room, deserted except for an occasional old soldier who saunters over for a beer or a coke. Most of the men are too old for anything stronger, and besides the Arizona night is too warm for serious drinking. I'm feeling ill-at-ease and uncomfortable in the summer weight blazer I'd grabbed hurriedly before leaving Chicago. The sleeves are too short and the waist too tight. I look and feel out of shape. I don't like not looking my best. I used to walk into the banquet rooms, exhilarated, feeling jaunty and trim after a hot shower and looking as slick as a tailor's dummy. I remember how my feet would do a quick shuffle in time to the music as I headed toward the bar.

I had been drinking beer most of the afternoon, but now, feeling as I did, I am in need of something stronger. I order a martini and survey the room looking for a place to sit. As I stand at the bar, I again ponder the question of how many more reunions are left in us. The men are old, worn out. I can see it in their faces. There have been too many deaths already, and more of us are likely to pass away within a few years. Our reunions are becoming little more than a death watch, a ghoulish game of waiting for a new batch of names to appear on a yellow sheet of paper.

As I have so often through the years, I think about Anita. In my mind, she is bound forever to our reunions as a result of those few hours I had spent with her long ago. She is my emotional link to the past — to my training days in California, to Joe Snopek and the rest of the men, to the Hollywood of old, to my youth and to every one of my memories of the war. But now even the memory of a woman I never really knew except as a fantasy has become so dim that I have trouble even remembering what she looks like.

I recall my trip home from Phil Rodriguez's funeral. There was time to kill at the L.A. airport before my plane took off for Chicago. I decided to try one more search of the L.A. phone book for someone, anyone, with Anita's maiden name, just as I had done so often before. Maybe there would be a new entry, a niece or nephew, a cousin, someone bearing the name Durchin who would eventually lead me to her. As I imagined it at the time, I would find a listing for the same last name. Then the voice on the other end of the line would say, "Oh yes, my Aunt Anita, let me give you a number where you can reach her. Durchin is not her name anymore, but I'm sure she'd be glad to hear from you, if you are who you say you are." My heart pounding, I would dial her number, and she would answer in that same sweet welcoming voice that I remembered from 1943, and she would be overjoyed to hear from me. She would recognize my voice instantly, and, as I imagined it, she would cover her mouth to stifle a scream. That's how happy she'd be to hear from me. Home is the warrior, home from the war, just five-and-a-half decades too late. She would be a widow by now, of course, and she would arrange to meet me at her home, and she would finally reveal to me that she had been praying that I would finally find her. We would sit on her sofa and talk excitedly, eager to cram in every detail of our lives since the war. Then, for old times' sake, we would return to where the Tail O'The Cock once stood on La Cienega, and we'd embrace, and then we would stroll past where the Brown Derby once stood, and in the warm summer evening we would hear someone singing "Sunday Monday or Always," and we would embrace again, oblivious to the traffic on Sunset Boulevard, not giving a damn about the stares of the passersby, for we would be lost in the middle of the sweetest reunion two old people could wish for.

But as I stood in the phone booth at LAX, the dream miraculously looked like it might come true. There, listed in the directory, was the name, Durchin. It had never appeared there before, not in all the years I'd been searching for it. The name was Jack Durchin. I blinked. It was no dream. I was not imagining it. I blinked again, just to make sure. My hand shaking I dialed the number. The phone rang, four, five times, then I heard the operator's voice. "That number has been disconnected," the recording said. I stood there for a moment, the receiver still in my hand. I continued standing at the phone, waiting for the news to sink in, and when it did, when I finally realized that the trail had come to an end and that I would never see her again, I slowly put the receiver back on the hook and walked to the gate to board my plane.

At the banquet, I find a table with an empty seat, and sit down next to Bruce Brodie and his wife, Colleen. Huey Long and his lady friend are also at the table. Looking around the room. I spot Charlie Murchison and Bo Smith seated separately, neither accompanied by his wife. Ed and Alma Soares are seated at a table with some C Battery men. I needn't have been concerned about my jacket. Very few men are wearing them. At one time, however, the men came dressed in their finest because there were but few occasions in life that could rival in importance those Saturday night reunion banquets. Furthermore, there were the group portrait sessions to consider. Before dinner, we would assemble in a separate room, all starched and solemn, our shoulders thrown back and stomachs tucked in, looking like a meeting of German *burgermeisters*. The photographer would arrange the group according to size, his pleas for us to smile going unheeded. Because for the last several years there haven't been enough men in attendance to afford the photographer, we now merely take snapshots of one another. I used to show them around in Chicago but they never evoked much interest. I've come to expect that, and today I toss them in a drawer and forget about them.

At our table, Huey Long's companion is telling me about traveling alone in an RV, but I am unmoved by her narrative. The deejay standing on the podium is playing melodies from the 1940's. The food had not been brought in, and the men, their wives and guests, are chatting as they nibble on their salads and hard rolls. The dance floor is as deserted as the bar.

A few decades back, at about this point, the men and their wives would crowd onto the dance floor. They would fall into each others' arms the moment the music started and glide across the floor as if their years of dancing together had magnetized them. Always in their midst was Master Sergeant Jim Mastropietro from Headquarters battery. He brought his wife to every reunion, and I doubt if he attended for any other reason than to dance. He was a quiet, polite Italian from Pennsylvania, a bit older than most of us. He never hung out around the bars or in the hotel restaurants, and I don't believe we ever exchanged a word, either during the war or at the reunions. But when the music began to play, Jim and his wife emerged, seemingly from nowhere, and spent the rest of the evening moving in tiny little steps across the floor like windup dolls. Then one year, not long ago, they stopped attending the reunions, leaving two empty places on the dance floor, and things weren't quite the same after that. I wanted to find out what happened to them but I wasn't sure who was still around who knew them that well. They had kept to themselves over the years, apparently staying in their room until it was time for the banquet, then suddenly to appear out of the mist like Veloz and Yolanda.

Besides simple good fellowship, dancing had always been the

big banquet attraction. The men and their wives were lured to the dance floor by the music they remembered from the past. At one time we had bands, and later on either a deejay or a trio, but there was always music, mostly ballads. On occasion some upbeat tunes had served to thin out the floor, causing some of the wives to cup their hands over their mouths in embarrassment as they hastily retreated to their tables.

Ed Soares ran the banquets, acting as impresario and master of ceremonies. He brought in singers and comics and, on one occasion, a former officer in the Luftwaffe as a guest speaker. Nearly every year, Tony and Kathy Rodrigues's daughter, a talented soprano, recited the Pledge of Allegiance and sang "America" and the "Star Spangled Banner." Whoever was the reunion chairman for that year made arrangements for the hotel or motel and selected the food. The food was usually simple fare, substantial and tasty and no one ever left the table hungry.

When the musicians took their break, it would be Charlie Murchison's turn. He would stand up in response to rollicking applause. He had an aw-shucks-guys way of acknowledging the ovation. Some of the men from A Battery, like myself, who had spent a lifetime listening to Charlie play, would begin chanting,

Before dinner, we would assemble, all starched and solemn, our shoulders thrown back and stomachs tucked in, looking like a meeting of German burgermeisters. (Reunion photograph, Chicago, circa 1955)

"Char-ley, Char-ley, Char-ley." And when the applause wouldn't let up, Charlie would spread his hands, palms up, and shrug, as if to say "well, if you want me to play that bad, what can I do?' And he would stride up to the piano with a big embarrassed grin, riffle the keys for a moment as if he were a Vegas dealer shuffling a deck of cards, and begin to play.

But on this night, I see no dancers, only a very ill Tony Rodrigues and an emaciated Alma Soares and a troubled Ed Soares, Ed's once proud handlebar moustache, thin and drooping. As I gaze around the room, I look over at Charlie, sitting quietly at his table, thinking no doubt of getting up early and driving his old blue pickup truck back to Oklahoma. I look around the room and see all my buddies, yesterday's warriors, looking as old and tired as I am, trying to give the reunion their last hurrah.

Then I remember my last conversation with Phil Rodriguez in Montebello. I had told him then that we will survive for only as long as there are reunions to attend; and when the reunions stop, the proud gunners of the 124th will be no more. Even though the reunions are coming to a close, how many other soldiers, I ask myself, can take away from a dying battalion so many memories, memories of the war, cruel as it may have been, memories of the men they had been close to since they were boys, and memories of girls named Anita, girls they scarcely knew but girls who, through their very connection to them, somehow got them through the war.

I decide to leave the banquet early. I take a few more bites of my food, and get up from the table. As I'm leaving, I stand for a moment by the door of the banquet room. Don Marks is on the podium singing, "I'm Stepping Out With A Memory Tonight." He's singing it slow and sad, just the way I like it.

APPENDIX

Surviving members
124th AAA Gun Battalion
(based on latest information available)

Headquarters Battery

AItieri, Raymond	West Haven, CT
Bilotta, Thomas J.	Louisville, KY
BIumeyer, Russel E.	Newton, IA
Bolen, Leland C.	Falls Church, VA
Conger, Charles W.	Madison, WI
Crnkovick, Jon J.	Chicago, IL
Dunn, Calvin	Springhill, IA
Flatley, Jerome B.	Mechanicsville, NY
Griesler, Bernard	North Platte, NE
Harmes, Lewis W.	Fort Wayne, IN
Hieser, Paul E.	Fostoria, OH
Holas, Gene	Tampa, FL
Holst, Jon J.	Washington, DC
Hornberger, Kenneth	Lawrence, KS
Johnson, Arlie L.	Rapid City, SD
Kidwell, John	Camp Spring, MD
Lanphear, Lowell	Paw Paw, MI
Mack, Millard	Sarasota, FL
Mastropietro, James J.	Bessmer, PA
McEvilly, James K.	Madison, WI
McLain, Dan L.	Sacramento, CA
Moon, Gerry	Sun City, AZ
Nott, Lloyd	Floyd, IA
Pike, Howard	Racine, WI

Rother, Phillip	San Diego, CA
Rudy, Charles A.	Williarnsport, MD
Schaffel, Edward	Mission Viejo, CA
Sell, Arnold	Wisconsin Rapids, Wl
Servey, Jose	San Diego, CA
Sottosanti, Alfred	Reno, NV
Stoner, Stewart	Reading, PA
Thompson, John E.	Santa Cruz, CA
Torpay Jr., John N.	North Arlington, NJ
Vandenberg, Melvin B.	Grand Rapids, MI
Wade, George W.	Matton, IL
Welch, Jack L.	Abilene, TX

A Battery

Abts, Clarence	Liberal, MO
Arcado, Anthony	Santa Rosa, CA
Armstrong, Robert	Tacoma, WA
Baca, Raul	San Francisco, CA
Bandur, Edwin	Genoa City, WI
Barker, Gene	Decherd, TN
Beimers, William	Grand Rapids, MI
Berzas, Lambert	Eunice, LA
Blackwell, Charles	Merced, CA
Blumenthal, Earl H.	Brooksville, FL
Brodie, Bruce	Champaign, IL
Borchardt, Laverne	Ft. Atkinson, WI
Brinegar, Pete	Duncan, OK
Brown, Stan W.	Sun City Center, FL
Calico, Gerald D.	Lancaster, CA
Carter, Lavone L.	Plano, TX
Costa, Neno	Fairfield, CA
Cummings, Edwin R.	Greenwell Springs, LA
Dias, Camerino	Lompoc, CA
Dickey. Robert E.	North Platte, NE
Dollar, Wayne	Marble Falls, TX
Durando, George J.	San Francisco, CA

Farrell, Gerald J.	Lincoln, NE
Goss, Bob	Chillicothe, MO
Grimes, Jesse L.	Anacortes, WA
Hanks, James L.	Noble, OK
Hill, Francis David	Bay City, MI
Hunter, Cortez	Lake Isabella, CA
Keck, Johnnie	West Columbia, TX
Klein Jr., Robert F.	Westwego, LA
Kranker,Rudy	Arma, KS
Kretschmer, Willis G.	Niles, IL
LeMaster, Dee	Amarillo, TX
Lim, Hong O.	San Francisco, CA
Loftin, Elvin	Sourlake, TX
Magliochetti, Anthony J.	Canoga Park, CA
Marks, Melvin	Chicago, IL
Matamoros, Marcellino	San Antonio, TX
Maxwell, Edward	Sarpeta, LA
Merlins, Terry	Racine, WI
Moyer, Ivan	Fulton, MI
Murabito, Joseph	New Buffalo. MI
Murchison, Charlie	North Tahlequah, OK
Musso, Carl	Aurora, CO
Nelson, Don B.	Denison, TX
Niccoli, John	Trinidad, CO
Oxford, Jim	Oxnard, CA
O'Brien, Francis J.	North Riverside, IL
Phillips, Theodore	North Glen, CO
Poche, Paul	Hanklinton, LA
Powell, James B.	Santa Maria, CA
Rangel, Santos H.	San Antonio, TX
Rhodes, Leon	East Tawes, MI
Sanchez, Frank	San Martin, CA
Saucedo, Juan	Del Rio, TX
Shaw, Harold	Sturtevant, WI
Silva, Don	Tahoe City, CA
Smith, Bowen N.	Palo Alto, CA

Smithson, Jack	Benton, AR
Thompson, Richard	North Platte, NE
Villanueva, Manuel	East Los Angeles, CA
Villareal, Guadalupe	Modesto, CA
Vodden, John	Los Gatos, CA
Willich, Clifford	Bouldenton, WI
Winkler, Chris	Waco, TX

B Battery

Allen, JC	Wenatchee, WA
Blundell, Layton	Paul Valley, OK
Bossier, Leonard H.	Alexandria, LA
Brigham, Dowayne	Litchfield, MI
Brown, Byron G.	West Sacramento, CA
Chapin, Hurbert R.	Lincoln, NB
Coller, Jay	Baldwin Park, CA
Cox, Ralph S.	Fair Hope, AL
Creecy, John P.	Bedford, TX
Delgadillo, Ben	Santa Maria, CA
Fields, Garland	La Pine, OR
Freeman, Charles	Santa Maria, CA
Geyer, Douglas	Big Bear Lake, CA
Gianelli, George	San Lorenzo, CA
Grijalva, George J.	Modesto, CA
Hansen, Karsten	Grass Valley, CA
Hein, Eugene E.	North Platte, NE
Hollaway, Rodney	Salinas, CA
Huffmyer, Milton L.	Las Cruces, NM
Jordan, R.G	Sourlake, TX
Ketterer, Joe H.	Scottsdale, AZ
Klatt, George W.	Clearlake, CA
Ladd, Hugh T.	Fosterville, MD
Lynch, Maurice J.	Sawners Grove, IL
Madak, John	Roseville, MI
Manord, Roy B.	Lafayette, IN
Marks, Don	South Euclid, OH

Mascias, Guillermo	Orlando, FL
Mashburn, Howard	Marietta, GA
Midkiff, Don E.	Kansas City, MO
Miller, John E.	Yucaipa, CA
Orvecz, Rudolph D.	Long Island, NY
Peterson, Charles J.	Regent, ND
Radford, Ralph W.	Murphy, NC
Ratto, Frank	Modesto, CA
Repetto, Roy	San Francisco, CA
Rodrigues, Tony	Hayward, CA
Salinas, Pedro	Oilton, TX
Silbert, Arvid	Sarasota, FL
Simionelli, Julius	Homewood, IL
Simpson, Leslie	Lakeside, CA
Singleton, T.E.	Tucson, AZ
Steffen, Carl R.	New Berlin, WI
Stelock, John	Falls Church, VA
Stenejen, Phillip	Williston, ND
West, Dale	Stanbury, MO
Williams, Floyd D.	Union, WA
Wright, Wendell W.	Oceanside, CA

C Battery

Allard, Roland	Pittsburgh, PA
Allen, Frank	Smithville, TX
Altergott, Bob	San Antonio, TX
Avila, Elroy	Donna, TX
Boles, Leslie	Caney, KS
Bradshaw, Herman	Morro Bay, CA
Contreras, Ysabel	Fresno, CA
Daprato, Willie	El Macero, CA
Dilsaver, KE	Altoona, PA
Eslyck, Lester L.	Pueblo, CO
Fratello, Frank	Los Angeles, CA
Glorius, Vincent	Ocala, FL
Gretsinger, Earl	Kenosha, WI

Griffun, Ralph	Moore, OK
Henderson, George A.	Baton Rouge, LA
Henderson, Lloyd	Enid, OK
Hester, Eiley F.	Gilroy, CA
Hodges, Glenn	Parnpa, TX
Hoyer, Charles D.	Loudonville, OH
Hoyt, Warren	Lansing, MI
Jansen, Robert A.	Collinsville, IL
Jiminez, Frank	Mountain View, CA
Joanis, Leroy B.	Long Beach, CA
Krieg, Fred	Ocala, FL
Kunz, Earl L.	Jamul, CA
Lee, Ben J.	North Platte, NE
Livingston, Ronald E.	Plainwell, MI
Logan, Wayne	Ellandale, MN
Martinez, Catarino J.	Stockton, CA
Massy, Robert D.	Macon, GA
Matheson, Walter L.	Gilroy, CA
McGuire, William F.	Mukwonago, WI
Mead, Raymond	Laverne, OK
Mishler, William L.	Hangerstown, MD
Modesti, Gustavo	San Francisco, CA
Olsen, Ralph	Vancouver, WA
Prosser, Robert	Minneapolis, MN
Pyle, Marion	El Dorado, AR
Quong, Kim	San Francisco, CA
Robarts, Milton E.	Portsmouth. NH
Sanders, John D.	Dallas, TX
Sharp, James T.	Chariton, IA
Shayer, Vince	Chicago, IL
Short, Edward	Nashville, TN
Smith, Richard	Lafayette, CA
Strutz, George	Murrieta, CA
Tapia Jr., Sam	Trinidad, CO
Thompson, Leo	Godfrey, IL
Trahern, Theodore F.	Collier, WY

Tunnell, Leonard H.	Miami, OK
Vangrow, Harold	Oak lawn, IL
Verbanac, Albert	Pear Blossom, CA
Ware, Vernon	San Antonio, TX
Watts, Jack	Victorville, CA
Webster, Don	Donavan, IL
Willardson, Russell	Parker, SD
Williams, Neil	Moreland, ID
Williarns, Rulen	Seattle, WA
Wilson, William O.	Bryson City, NC

D Battery

Aguilar, Joe	El Paso, TX
Bacon, John	Daytona Beach, FL
Baker, Jr., Roy	Calville, WA
Baron, Gene	Gridley, CA
Bartolf, George	Royal Oak, MI
Cade, Carl	Wichita, KS
Connor, Dave	Dorris,CA
Correnti, Sam	Rockford, IL
Danik, George	Arkon, OH
Delabio, Elmer	Kenosha, WI
Dobrovolny, Joe	Ross, ND
Frugoli, Julius	Capitola, CA
Gaona, Dan	San Antonio, TX
Hickey, Dennis	Putney, VT
Hoff, Oroville	Rockford, IL
Holland, Edwin	Stonewall, OK
Jantz, Danver	Lubbock, TX
Johnson,Leee	Rockford, IL
Jolly, Donald	Corpus Christi, TX
Jones, Robert	Gadson, AL
Kelly, Edward	Bay City, MI
Krizay, Ed	Las Vegas, NV
Lear, Leonard	Lincoln, NB
LeDoux, Pat	Roy, NM

Leighton, Harold	Blanchard, OK
Long, Alvin	Chandler, AZ
Martinez, Pifanio	La Junta, CO
Martinez, Tony	Houston, TX
Martinez, Rubel	Las Vegas, NV
Mason, WM	Norwalk, CA
Michaels, James	Stockton, CA
Murray, Ed	Napa, CA
Rizos, Wm	Delcanto, MD
Russell, Forrest	Fullerton, CA
Sarubi, Peter	Sonoma, CA
Smellgrove, Garrett	Ozark, AK
Soares, Ed	Hayward, CA
Stefani, Hank	Post Falls, ID
Tucker, HK	Summerville, GA
Vitale, Chris	Santa Clara, CA
Vize, HR	Alton, IL
Watson,Wm.	Sonoma,CA
Williams, JT	Tempe, AZ